CW00554414

The Concept of Time and Historical Experience

The Concept of Time and Historical Experience

By

Mihai Popa

Cambridge
Scholars
Publishing

The Concept of Time and Historical Experience

By Mihai Popa

This book first published 2023

Cambridge Scholars Publishing

Lady Stephenson Library, Newcastle upon Tyne, NE6 2PA, UK

British Library Cataloguing in Publication Data
A catalogue record for this book is available from the British Library

ISBN (10): 1-5275-3715-3
ISBN (13): 978-1-5275-3715-6

To professor Alexandru Surdu
(1938–2020)

TABLE OF CONTENTS

PREFACE

For more than 2500 years, history has remained an intriguing subject for European culture and a point of interest that has either brought great minds together or quite the contrary, it has alienated the most brilliant minds by sealing the peoples' destinies through political decisions. It seems that both possibilities got inspired by the truly subjective quality of man's encounter with the deep reality of his becoming, in which he wants to include everything that ever belonged to him within time, especially his experience with time. Reason forces time to fit into its patterns and suit this reality. Thus, when investigated, it becomes an abstraction. Man often forgets that he himself is time and that the most natural attitude towards it is to just let it run its course. There is no need to research time. Better yet, instead of confronting it, one must let time reveal itself. By allowing time to find you, you are meeting yourself somewhere in between the road towards understanding at any cost (especially at the cost of sufficient reason) and comprehending the communion with yourself, the closest, yet the furthest fellow we have got in history; this communion does not fade in time (in history), but on the contrary, it is our purpose – meeting our being.

We judge history from many different perspectives; we slice and divide it, and look for its principles and meanings, but we never let it forget us. According to Constantin Noica, when entering history, man does not want to forget, but the purpose of history, the reality of the *historical act* is precisely the act of forgetting. It is a synthesis of time. Seeing things from this perspective, the researcher's attitude (philosopher, historian, sociologist, anthropologist etc.) is that of a person wanting to forget while preserving what is relevant to humanity. Unlike the study object of science, the historical fact cannot be handled and moved as an object towards the epistemic subject, even though both are entities dominated by becoming and they have entered temporality. We subjectively manifest within the object of science while we attempt to catch the essence of this reality, which is the law or the universal. In the meantime, two types of subjectivity overlap within historical facts. The reason why history seems unstable is that as man moves forward in time, he also leaves the impression that he moves away from these temporal realities: the present, the time of his actions, and the historical present he only thinks about. Man wishes nothing else but to keep them. The reality of the researcher does not coincide with the reality of a fact experienced by someone else in a different time, and both realities can confess and are deeply and hopelessly humane. Historical experience belongs to the historical time when people enter a communion and share their victories, fears and truths – which have no time – and the desire (the will to exist within history) to accomplish within becoming more than the becoming is pouring into mankind: the reason for existing within history. According to Noica, behind every philosophy, there is an *ingenium perenne,* the gate towards facing the world before becoming the thought of reason in conversation with itself, motivated to appoint a *philosophia perenuis.*

We take Noica's question from *How is something new possible* and ask how it is possible for the spirit not to become redundant then we return it with a different meaning to history and to the experience gained while becoming within history. We ask: how is it possible for man, always new, to recognize himself inside history? A few thousand years of history cannot lead to a self-encounter nor to losing ourselves in the world according to the meaning we give or not to the historical experience.

This meaning is part of recapturing the human essence, no matter how many avatars it had to climb. Do we unify our present time with the permanence we seek inside history? And how else do we look for it either than through dialogue? What we search for in history is the connection with the universal man that inhabits each of us. Communion becomes a vivid history whose meaning unravels for us now, although we have forgotten it: time is no longer seen just as a rigid straightness but as a network of possibilities and historical meanings dialectically gathered to carry our message through time.

If we continue to comprehend time as a rigid one-way direction, forever lost in the immensity of space and think about succession without any connection we will become victims of history and risk remaining outside of it. Noica is right in not denying history to philosophy but differently: he does not contradict its becoming, just the becoming for the sake of becoming: "A history that explains the phenomena or one in which they explain themselves will portray them in a succession and their determinism if it is possible. But it is a virtue peculiar to the history of philosophy to be able to follow, more than the assimilation of the products portrayed by the spirit its inner necessities." (*Sketch for the history of How is something new possible*, p. 13–14). Starting from this reality of philosophical thought, we tried to reach an inner necessity of historical thought. Thus, we are trying to draw the coordinates of a possible experience for the man inside history. Experience seen in direct correlation to historical fact is a theory derived from the philosophy of the Stagirite. Experience connects us to the raw deed, the experienced moment of life. The author of *Metaphysics* also says that the universal exists within and through the individual. In this case, the historical fact is not an individual but becomes a historical universal that belongs to everyone, and we rediscover ourselves in it: it is both a confession and a temporal connection. To overcome the straightness that does not inflect but alienates the deeds of the spirit by weakening the meaning of becoming, we need to return historical experience to its initial form: the communion of the being with itself inside the historical time. This way, time and history interblend and bring the deed into the present time of each thought. Having only this as a starting point, history does not intend to give the present time back to the time of each period because it cannot. No matter how much it tries, it will still be present in its *own time* inside the historical time. If it can find what Noica calls "that principle that keeps on giving itself – the spirit" within history and philosophy, it could re-establish the dialogue between history and the historical being.

The author

ACKNOWLEDGMENTS

The issue of this book would not have been possible without the constant and competent support of some people I want to take the opportunity now to thank:

First of all, I would like to thank my wife, Adriana, for her patience, suggestions, encouragement and affection, in the absence of which I would not have been able to finish these pages.

I would also like to thank Ms Floriana Stavarache, who translated this text into English and was able to choose the most suitable words and phrases to match the meaning of some specific connotations in Romanian, the original language of the text.

Another thank you goes to Ms Daniela Florescu for editing the whole book.

Finally, a special thank you to the team working at Cambridge Scholars Publishing for its professional and yet friendly encouragement, as well as for providing me with useful suggestions throughout the entire process of publishing this book.

Mihai Popa

CHAPTER I

TIME AND ETERNITY: ANTHROPOLOGICAL MODELS OF INSERTION IN TIME

Retrieved time and the historical chronotropy

There is a conflict emerging regularly within those societies determined to 'evolve' in time and to 'create' history, and it manifests between the time of becoming and the time of Creation. Mircea Eliade[1] did a lengthy analysis of this phenomenon. The eternal return, passing through different cycles in history, all of it takes into account the purpose of the universal Creation. Nothing gets achieved outside of this purpose. The things, the beings and the society man lives in and creates bear the symbol of Creation and the desire to acquire knowledge about it. Time no longer represents an indifferent shape for man, but it is this exact time when a deed, a thing or an experience gains significance in connection to a different time, the initial one of the Creation. It represents an indestructible bond between two moments, the current one and the one revealed in *illo tempore*. This bond created man, as it itself is a revelation of the sacred. [2] We will not follow a straight path in Eliade's footsteps because we also have other theories available and notions used by great thinkers to underline the specificity of the relation between time and history.

The conceptualization of time and how man (as an individual or a society) relates to time strictly depends on culture. We cannot understand the concepts of time or experiencing time outside a cultural model. Time – also a cultural model – cannot exist outside society, just as society cannot be conceived outside of time. Time patterns, their concepts and the cultures

---

[1] Mircea Eliade, *The Myth of The Eternal Return,* translated from French by Willard R. Trask (New York: Harper&Brathers Publishers, 1959).
[2] Mircea Eliade, *Sacred and The Profane. The Nature of Religion*, translated from French by Willard R. Trask (New York: Harcourt, Brace&World, Inc., 1959), pp. 99-113.

they are born in and which they represent form together a historical and cultural chronotropy. This concept comes from physiology and refers to the regularity and frequency of a rhythm (cardiac, anabolism-catabolism, reproductive etc., < from the French *cronotrope*). Using this concept to historically assess the cultural rhythms is not an exaggerated analogy because, in the life of society, there are certain essential rhythms that regulate it. There are general and individual rhythms, some that configure it and some that define it, or just unspecified ones that contradict the normal life rhythm of society, affecting its functions or even destroying it.

The *cronotrope* and *chronotropy* of a society (culture) represent a synthesis of rhythms, just like they would inside an organism, and this is fully justified if we keep in mind that in a society or a culture, similar to an organism or biotope, there are general and individual times, specific and non-specific times, as well as rhythms and tempos that intersect and collaborate to create a unique rhythm, proper to that precise organism or culture. So we can understand this concept as universal or particular, general or individual. There are also typical rhythms and atypical ones. If an atypical rhythm intervenes inside a system (let's say an organism), unfit for how it organises its vital functions, it can disturb its fundamental rhythms and finally lead to its dissolution or even death. Examining the principles and emphasizing the rhythms of a society or culture can be done using either universal or particular tropes, as well as contradicting tempi or colliding rhythms which oppose each other when they are not working together to maintain life. This reality of rhythms renders time not as much of a form of the universal becoming perceivable in one dimension and having a unique meaning, but rather as a more complex reality or form. To quote Vulcănescu, 'for Romanians, time has density, as well as content'[3].

The science of rhythms (the Greek *rhytmos*), specific to arts as well, represents the expression of a much deeper reality, and has been a preoccupation of those with a higher level of spirituality, especially

---

[3] 'Time has its particular dimensions. At first glimpse, time seems to have only one dimension: length. Things are placed one after another, thus forming a row, so the length of time appears as the only available dimension. After a closer look, time also has volume, meaning consistency. The world exists all at once, like the inclusion of many things given simultaneously, where all things have their own strings of specific successive events. [...] In reality, the world has all the dimensions of space, plus its progression in time. Therefore, time is nothing other than the world in a process of becoming, so for Romanians is not just a string, but also a content.' Quote from Mircea Vulcănescu, *Dimensiunea românească a existenței* (The Romanian Dimension of Existence), edition supervised by Marin Diaconu (Bucharest: Publishing of the Romanian Cultural Foundation, 1991), p. 104.

scientists and philosophers. In Romanian culture, only three great thinkers have turned rhythm (successions, vibrations, waves) into forms of expression and analysis, the fundamental principles of thought, existence and history: Vasile Conta, A. D. Xenopol and Vasile Pârvan. Concerning the last one (because the exegesis and the analysis of the first two are at hand) we should mention the importance the historical rhythm had, not just in one lecture, but in all of his work:

> Within the infinity of variations of the cosmic rhythm lays the rhythm of human life, just like a lost note in the symphony of spheres. It is unique. Its shapes seem to create just as many diverse rhythms, but it is just an opinion. It is the rhythm of spiritual life: it goes up and down in steady beats, hurrying up or being late, in harmony or counterpoint, as categorical and fatal in art as in politics, in science as in religion, in economy as in philosophy. The rhythm of human life seen through its different spiritual becomings is the historical rhythm. Just like there is no body without a space, there is no spirit without a rhythm. The evolution of the human spirit is the history of a creative life's rhythm. The Romanian culture is rhythm solidified in actions. One can find rhythm by researching actions.[4]

The importance of rhythm, and in a more profound cultural and scientific way, the importance of chronotropy will be revealed when we will take into consideration the different *anthropological models of time insertion.*

For starters, we should make some preliminary observations regarding the relationship between temporal rhythms and the historical becoming, seen as an answer to the present historical challenges. Further on, we will expand this observation to the longer-lasting stages. Using these observations, we could also analyse the different theoretical or cultural, and historical approaches of the chronotropy as a reaction to the activity of universal time, cosmic time and historical time. Different perspectives have risen different analyses of the temporal model, either cultural anthropology, historiography or the history of philosophy. The first observation that stood out to researchers and has contributed to a deeper understanding of the relationship between time and history is the connection between cosmic and

---

[4] Vasile Pârvan, *Scrieri alese, Studii şi eseuri,* III. *Despre ritmul istoric* (Selected Works, Studies and Essays, III. On the Historical rhythm), opening lesson from the lecture on *Istoria religiunilor* (The History of Religions), held during the summer semester MCMXX at the University of Bucharest, read on the 4th of February MCMXX), introduction and notes by Alexandru Zub, preface (for the princeps edition) by Radu Vulpe (Bucharest: Publishing of the Romanian Academy, 2006), p. 535.

historic time. This connection was possible by questioning the bond between *time* and *eternity* – a tradition in metaphysics. For anthropology, ethnography and the entire prehistoric archaic mentality, the pattern of cosmic time was primordial. Actually, it appeared – how else – when man began to conceptualize the time of the historical becoming. This pattern's mark is the need for a centre (symbolical, archetypal) of creation.

Ancient societies have developed quite the symbolism for the centre. That is the symbol of time and space, with the role of a cosmogonic principle. The temple and the altar are in the centre; people gather all around it. Cosmic time is a recurrent time.

> To us, it seems an inescapable conclusion that *the religious man sought to live as near as possible to the Centre of the World.* He knew that his country lay at the midpoint of the earth; he knew too that his city constituted the navel of the universe and, above all, that the temple or the palace were veritably Centres of the World. But he also wanted his own house to be at the Centre and to be an *imago mundi.* '[5]

We might say that within the cosmologic paradigm of the universal becoming, time goes back to eternity because it is not identical to becoming, nor eternity is equal to the lack of motion. Eternity can be the undefined duration of a moment, the present taking over the past and the future or a permanent present in which everything is born, like in Plato or Plotinus. Noica's concept of becoming within being carries within the image of Plato's dialectics, where everything individual tends to assign itself traits able to pull it out of the irrational that lays within a becoming for the sake of becoming and redirect it towards the rational becoming *within being.*

> As I see it, then, we must begin by making the following distinction: What is that which always is and has no becoming, and what is that which becomes but never is? The former gets grasped by understanding, which involves a reasoned account. It is unchanging. The latter gets grasped by opinion, which involves unreasoning sense perception. It comes to be and passes away, but never really is. Now everything that comes to be must of necessity come to be by the agency of some cause, for nothing can come to be without a cause.[6]

---

[5] M. Eliade, *Sacred and The Profane. The Nature of Religion,* 1959, p. 43.
[6] Plato, *Timaeos,* translated by Donald J. Zeyl, in *idem, Complete Works,* edited, with Introduction and Notes, by John M. Cooper, associate editor D.S. Hutchinson (Indianapolis/Cambridge: Hacket Publishing Company, 1997), p. 1234, 28 a-b.

The centrality of the universe is ontological. By definition, centrality is spatial. But this centrality has repercussions on time, and the event registers within a circular duration. Consequently, the major events, sacred, symbolic and with an ontological value, can escape regular time, properly historical. The circular ontological time is sacred.

> One essential difference between these two qualities of time strikes us immediately: *by its very nature, sacred time is reversible* in the sense that, properly speaking, it is *a primordial mythical time made present.* Every religious festival, any liturgical time, represents the re-actualization of a sacred event that took place in a mythical past, "in the beginning." Religious participation in a festival implies emerging from ordinary temporal duration and reintegration of the mythical time re-actualized by the festival itself. Hence sacred time is indefinitely recoverable and indefinitely repeatable. [7]

Man truly lives within the sacred time, and he tries to ignore the historical one, which he needs to pass through – a historical necessity – and which he also regularly tries to obliterate, but actually succeeds in doing so only within the time and space of a religious celebration.

> Hence religious man lives in two kinds of time, and the most important, sacred time, appears under the paradoxical aspect of a circular time, reversible and recoverable, a sort of eternal mythical present that periodically reintegrates using rites. [8]

This 'waiver' from the historical event, man's refusal of the time that pulls him outside the horizon of the sacred event, has been of great importance in the period between wars in Romania. Escaping and denying history is specific only to Eliade, and we can notice this attitude in most thinkers who had Nae Ionescu as a mentor. The periodicity of the sacred event, and rethinking the significance of mythology in most nations are subjects that spiked Eliade's interest in particular. Rethinking the historical event and the specific time of historical becoming, even if not from a speculative-metaphysical perspective, is something we find in Constantin Noica, Mircea Vulcănescu or Emil Cioran. One way or another, historical time is theorized, valued and turned into a symbol inside the horizon of the historical event. There is e certain bipolarity, especially theoretical, between event and historical time, but also an intrinsic specificity of the time-event relation in history, which is reflected by the definition of historical time. This way of approaching history and events in connection with time and its

---

[7] M. Eliade, *Sacred and The Profane. The Nature of Religion,* 1959, pp. 68-69.
[8] Ibid., p. 69.

particular historical significance (related to the true *historical* event) has
been considered a touchstone by historians, philosophers or simple narrators
of history. Nicolae Iorga found himself in a continuous argument with
historians writing 'histories' without substance, making rather literature on
the event and ignoring the essence of the historical becoming, thus exiting
the time of the event that had historical significance. He was trying to pull
history from under the temptation of 'romanticizing', always referencing
the event from the sources and its authenticity, recovered or not by critics.
He pleaded for history written based on the historical fact and not about it,
for a 'historiology' able to provide 'with or without introducing the critique,
the overwhelming whole of the sources that give, through their
contemporary status, a colour and a freshness that the historian's literary
talent would never be able to reproduce.' [9]

Historians understood first and better the bond between event and time
or the chronology of the historical deed because they were closer to the
sources narrating it. Philosophers mostly speculated about time and
understood it ontologically, but less historically. Thus, they were unable
to study it within the horizon of the event. Time has no logic when
separated from the event, so if logic is lost, only the 'times' detached from
events remain. When time is detached from the event, it becomes an empty
abstraction – useful in discourse – and attempting to fill it with something
will only lead to another abstraction, ontologically complementary to
time: space. H. Bergson tried to correct this inconvenience through the
concept of duration. We can configure a chronotype from within the
horizon of an event because time does not appear to be passing in one
direction as a continuous string. Chronotropy (Greek *cronos* = time,
trópos = way) sees the event plenary, intersecting with time (in reality,
with times), where different rhythms, longer or shorter, closer or farther
away, resonate to create an action. If we visually represent the *cronotrope*,
unseparated from the event and at the intersection of rhythms, we obtain
a lens-like representation of the event determined by time. The past and
the future are no longer lines intersecting in the present, and they become
intersecting spheres.

---

[9] Nicolae Iorga, *Permananţele istoriei* (The Permanences of History), speech held
at The International History Congress in Zürich, september, 1938, in *Generalităţi cu
privire la studiile istorice* (General ideas on historical studies), 3rd edition
(Bucharest: The Institute of Universal History „N. Iorga" , 1944), p. 239.

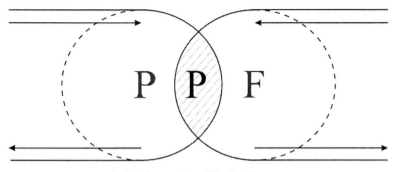

Graphical Representation of Historical Chronotropy
P Past
P – Present
F – Future

The surface within the shaded interior of the intersection of the two spheres represents the *cronotrope*, with the two hemispheres forming the horizons of the event: posterior and anterior. Such a representation offers the possibility to imagine the actual event as a complex of possibilities produced from both the harmonics previously prefigured, done in the present and the bonds anticipated through the expectancy horizon of any event. This way, present time gains amplitude, content and direction, while it also suggests a dynamic and permanent retroversion due to the authenticity of the event being in a permanent tension between the spheres of incidence where rhythms interblend and get anticipated.

This visual representation was suggested by the 'volume', meaning the content of the temporal dimension captured by Vulcănescu in his ontology of time for Romanians. [10] The complexity of the temporal models suggested here intuitively gains new dimensions by integrating cultural models when we are right in the field of historical events.

Lucian Blaga paid special attention to stylistic factors in defining the historical being, which only has significance as the revealing of a mystery able to 'move' the event from the temporal-historic transition into the existence of the deed as history:

> [...] a historical knowledge fully attains its objective when it manages to reveal not just the emergence, duration and disappearance in space and time

---

[10] Mircea Vulcănescu, *Dimensiunea românească a existenţei* (The Romanian Dimension of Existence), 1991 , pp. 104 – 105.

of historical actions, but especially when it manages to shed light on the stylistic aspects that characterize these actions. [11]

There are times and ways of perceiving temporality. Each thing has its own history, but we only perceive its present time right here, even though we can think of it as consecution, a reunion of previous factors and just as many moments that have determined it. Everything has a story that does not coincide with its linear and unique history because that is not its complete history. There are as many times as there are consciousnesses, but time itself is a combination of rhythms or a purposeful path within a network of events; inside this network, the event is a knot connecting the past with the future; anterior and posterior are relative landmarks for a *right now* that has already disappeared as soon as we believe it got set. We talk about times and places inflicted with the mentioned time, but we rarely pay the deserved attention to the relative time of a place because we imagine time as a sovereign, identical to itself in any of its segments, regardless of space. At least, this is how science sees it, singling out just the succession and its direction. Time can deform space; man and things bend before time, as it is not an indulgent sovereign, but unmerciful and oppressive. It is just an illusion that time works in our favour. That is why humans have imagined a time machine.

The Evolution of the Idea of Freedom. Freedom is a privilege gained in time; it does not become it exists. Only our concept of freedom changed. The connection of time with history, seen through the perspective of all the changes endured after better constitutions and written or non-written settlements, does not involve a becoming of the concept of freedom. Freedom exists or not; it can be hidden or revealed in ideas. Nicolae Iorga tells us how can *our* notion of freedom *evolve*, how it appears or disappears wrapped in regulations or rendered by decrees. He does not use a philosophical definition, but its historical meaning, taking into consideration its moral function, the cultural ideals, the political target and even the economic necessity of each epoch. [12] For him, time binds everything and gathers in its stream ideas from different historical spaces, not so foreign or impenetrable regarding the lifestyle and even less regarding the world and life in general. Of course, this is not a new perspective. Hegel himself – which Iorga had read, just as he had read and appreciated Xenopol – understood the becoming of Idea as a way for the

---

[11] Lucian Blaga, *Fiinţa istorică* (The Historical Being), supervised edition, notes and preface by Tudor Cătineanu (Cluj-Napoca: Dacia Publishing, 1977), p. 191.

[12] Nicolae Iorga, *Evoluţia ideii de libertate* (The Evolution of the Idea of Freedom), supervised edition, introductive study and notes by Ilie Bădescu (Bucharest: Meridiane Publishing, 1987), p. 65.

Spirit to manifest into the world. Yet the novelty lies in the manner of modifying everlasting ideas emerging from doctrines or born out of the interest of some cults. The ability to change these ideas proves there is movement, spiritual becoming and exchanges between apparently distant societies, not just in space, but also in time. As an example, we can consider the evolution of the Christian idea of freedom and the entire subtle transition (contradictory as well) of Christianity throughout the first centuries under the Roman tradition. To understand the phenomenon brought about by the social transformation of the spirit of freedom and religious tolerance under the influence of an ideology, we must also consider the intolerance imposed by the Judaic caste of priests in doctrinaire issues. This opportunity arose due to the Roman conquest. Reforming the Hebrew religion would not have been possible if the priests of the Jerusalem Temple had not conceded to the Roman administrative reform (opposition would have actually been impossible under political and military reign). The Romans themselves, as polytheist people, were in favour of the religions adopted by the conquered territories as long as they did not interfere with the official cult of the emperor, as well as the administrative organization. However, when the Western civilisation (the Romans) encountered the oriental one, represented by the Hellenistic culture and the influences of the religious beliefs brought on by the new cults, arrived with the new administration and especially the occupying army, it was almost impossible to isolate people based on their beliefs. 'If it had not been for this mixed dough of Hellenistic Judaism compliant with the Roman dominion and their proconsuls at the fore, and if Jerusalem was that of the single Levites, then the temple would have been quickly shut by scared priests so that nothing coming from the far sun of this new religion could get in' [13] (Christianity – our note, M. P.).

These changes require many factors; besides the political, economic and cultural, there are also temporal ones. Each religion (not to mention the economical 'technique', even the political and ideological in applying it) also implies different ways of managing time. Iorga does not insist on this necessity to coordinate temporal factors but it exists and is presumed by a historian, if not explicitly seen. The fact is, behind any affirmation stating a change, of any kind, there is also a specific time. The Roman spirit, innovative in certain fields (art, ideology) and conservative in others (administrative technique, morals and especially law), represents the temporality of an organized deed, almost turned into law – regarding the law and the administrative system etc. The Judaic spirit had a different temporal dimension, 'canonized' in the revealed texts representing one field

---

[13] Ibid., p. 126.

of the sacred, where the time of the revelation was one-way directed, and revelation itself was 'a contract' between divinity and the chosen people.

There is also another time, circular, represented by Hellenistic polytheism and the Indo-Aryan, Brahmanic and Buddhist religions in particular.

For the Romans, the pragmatic spirit (sometimes utilitarian) managed time, while for the Judeans, time had a historical dimension above all, and they were the first people to deliberately accept history as a way to 'consume' a divine promise. According to Judeans, the historical time gains a revelatory dimension,[14] something that does not happen in other cultures where revelation does not require a human existence historically involved, but on the contrary, it can occur within the cosmic time, of a cyclical fashion.

> Judaism represents a massive innovation compared to the archaic and paleo-oriental religions or the mythical and philosophical ideas of the Eternal Return, as elaborated in India and Greece. *For Judaism, Time has a beginning and also an end.* The notion of cyclical time has been exceeded. Yahweh no longer manifests in *Cosmic Time* (like the gods of other religions) butwithin a *Historical Time,* which is irreversible.[15]

However, the Hellenistic time was in a different cultural (and historical) phase compared to the classical and cyclic time, organized by classical philosophies like Platonism. The Macedonian conquest of the Orient represented not just an occasion for cultural and religious syncretism but also a major temporal debilitation which later will set the basis for a smooth incorporation of Christianity. The paradigm of Greek time, through its Platonic, Neoplatonic and even Aristotelian doctrine, continued to influence the Christian ideology even in its elaborated form imposed by the fathers of the church, and its essence was abandoned ever since medieval times. This rejection, even if not entirely, became noticeable in the modern era. The Creation was regularly brought back to life, just like Plato presented it in the myth of the destroyed Universe, yet periodically rebuilt by the Demiurge and got replaced by a new 'movement' in the post-Napoleon era. This movement sometimes had a pregnant catastrophic look, especially in the scientific theories, like the one belonging to Cuvier. Lucian Blaga also described the changes in the classical temporal paradigm, including its Platonic reminiscences, briefly but very suggestive, through *the style of the romantic culture.*

---

[14] M. Eliade, *Sacred and The Profane*, 1959, p. 92.
[15] Ibid., pp. 103 – 104.

Time and everything related manifested a profound inclination towards "movement". God himself was taken down and placed on the barricades at the becoming of history. The Platonic "ideas" were leaving Mount Olympus, allowing change, action and the storm. No wonder Cuvier imagined the earth going through catastrophes followed by new creations. In the political life of the continent, the revolts and rebellions came one after another, just like the "punches" and "creations" of the geological conception of the great scientist. [16]

The already mentioned example, this time coming from a much further historical context than the moment we started in, is very significant concerning how the value of a temporal (cosmologic and cyclic) paradigm contributes to the restructuring of a traditional theoretical vision of time while coming in contact with a modern one. The time of 'establishing' the Christian spirit within history, together with its perspective on temporality (historical and cosmic) and similar to the concept of liberty, gains new value in Iorga's analysis. That was possible because, during the first decades and centuries, Christianity had to recover, not just after all the different cultural and religious doctrines (especially Greek, Roman and Hebrew) but also because of the convergence of the times implied by these doctrines and cultures. That becomes obvious for us when Iorga brings into discussion the influence of the Aryan spirit along with its temporal factor intertwined in its spirituality, the cult models and the social reality. Within the life of the Brahmanic society, despite the caste spirit, there was a certain liberty cultivated, also reflected in the Vedic literature. Their worship style offered a certain liberty of the spirit. Indian literature stands as proof of this. *The Ramayana, The Mahabharata*, theatre and poetry are open to the cosmic miracle and the beauties of continuously changing nature. 'This is not a religious theatre, with vultures circling above like the first Greek tragedy in which actors appear as gods [...]. The Indian theatre has something free, open in front of nature, humane.' [17] Nevertheless, the Indic mentality was missing forms strictly regulated for a doctrine, the vectors of revealed faith. Despite the caste barriers, there were some sort of tendencies, if we cannot call them values, to render religion more democratic, and they started circulating right when Buddhism emerged. 'The last pariah is as close to Buddha's heart as the proudest member of Kshatriya, or the 'most saint' of the Brahmins.' [18] While the 'customs' of the Judean tradition have been shaped by clergymen – more often than not under political influence –, Buddhism is tolerant of cult issues:

---

[16] L. Blaga, *Fiinţa istorică* (The Historical Being), 1977, p. 111.
[17] N. Iorga, *Evoluţia ideii de libertate* (The Evolution of the Idea of Freedom), 1987, p. 122.
[18] Ibid., p. 124.

the believer can choose his/her way towards salvation and the path towards
the divine spirit. Buddhist humility transforms the social rhythm into a time
of communication going downwards and upwards between the divine
authority and the believer. According to Iorga, the suffering implied by the
Christian message recommended to both masters and the subdued as a
purpose or a path towards redemption was one form of the compassion
preached by the scripture, but also *an entirely Indian trait* assimilated by the
Christian doctrine on its way to get established. If Brahmanism was
obedience, Buddhism pleaded for kinship and sympathy, changing the
meaning of existence and divine revelation. This incipient humanism
represented a new form of spiritual freedom and has influenced, directly or
indirectly, the faith in Christ. There are many similarities between the moral
beliefs preached by the scriptures and the humane conceptions of Buddha's
followers:

> And then the king's son transforms and becomes everyone's man, of every
> pain and instead of seeing that horrible caste of clergymen, in front of which
> everybody trembled as they had the members of the Kshatriya with their
> swords on their left and right, then some poorly kept monks started walking
> among them, eaten by disease and needs, without fortunes and barely
> dragging their bloody feet on the ground; a sort of barefoot Franciscan of the
> Middle Ages.[19]

The new Christian religion flourishes on its own and has its own time, a
time of the man, recovered from history; throughout history, it continues to
gather many other temptations that place doubt on it. Its true liberty is not the
one based on doctrinaire forms. The Roman Empire ensured this kind of
'liberty' through religion (political, actual), introduced in its space of interest.
Early on, the Greeks did it differently, by placing value on some more
elevated forms of spiritual culture. One way or another, time configures these
values, but it also makes them go out of fashion. The Christian message
helped separate the political form from the one beyond time represented by
divine grace under one condition: *participation* out of love. That could have
been the condition (and, in reality, it was) of every great culture, precisely
how not long ago, it was the Greek one. Even though Jesus was not imposing
anything – besides loving thy neighbour – the perspective of almost endless
freedom within the human condition could have had a moral limitation
beyond its temporal one: 'In manifesting this liberty no injustice should occur,
and no pain awaken.'[20]

---

[19] Ibid., p. 125.
[20] Ibid., p. 128.

This example partially illustrates the confluence of historical facts distant in space and time but brought together by their significance in human ontology, which foreshadows a new event (the emergence of Christianity). The concept of freedom is the constant element. There are also the time constants of the chronotype initiated through the synthesis of different rhythms, as well as some about time, specific to the cultural areas brought on by history, able to open up the perspective for the new event. All these spiritual and historical connections have their *model of insertion in time:* The Indian one, particular to the Brahmanic and Buddhist spirituality; the Greek one, rigorously structured and extremely rational, which had already taken on several changes through the oriental intrusion during the Hellenistic period; the Roman one, in full ascent, pragmatically and able to civilize by definition; the Judean one, similarly well-organized that fully values history. Judeans bring forth a linear and irreversible historical determinism, based on which every important event is the will of Yahweh. We can even state that Judean spirituality presents the concept of a historical destiny different from how it was understood by the Greeks, from a substantial perspective (the path of each – human or collective – is pre-established in its essence and will necessarily get realised despite any obstacle. This concept is also illustrated by the myth of Oedipus, among others.). The infiltration of Judeans within the horizon of history makes it possible for a revelation to happen *in historical times.*

> For Judaism, the time has a beginning and will have an end. The idea of cyclic time is left behind. Yahweh no longer manifests himself in cosmic time (like the gods of other religions) but in a historical time, which is irreversible. Each new manifestation of Yahweh in history is no longer reducible to an earlier manifestation.[21]

Historical Chronotropy and Social Entropy

Let us interpret each social-historical event as a synthesis of some spiritual and humane vectors inside a culture, restraining the social entropy based on a cultural model of historical existence. The consciousness organizes reality according to its categories, culturally generated. It does not double the existence but coordinates it based on experience; it does not govern it (like a cause-effect type of relation) but *knows* it and creates its spiritual world based on it and inside of it. We do not raise the issue of spiritual metaphysics for now, just that of an ontological history. From the perspective of consciousness (seen in general, the transcendental one, according to Kantian apriorism), time

---

[21] M. Eliade, *Sacred and The Profane*, 1959, p. 110.

is a category of the sensitive intuition given *a priori* and not resulting from either interior or exterior experience; time and space are forms preceding experience, based on which we can organize it. At this stage, by being pure intuition preceding experience, the transcendental theory of time brings something extra to the notion of time in comparison to that of space: we can ignore space for the internal phenomena of the consciousness, but we cannot do the same with time because it is one-dimensional, infinite and one-directional. There is just one uniform infinite time (according to Newton's physics); more times are parts of the same time. All of these data come from the critique of Rădulescu-Motru on the transcendental time,[22] meant to do one thing: introduce the notion of *destiny* as the philosopher understands it. In reality, this notion – introduced by Motru in the context of his philosophy of energetic personalism – has its origins in some older attempts of the ancient Greeks to define the concept of time. For them, it was established on the physical notion of movement, introduced by philosophy, and it will end up in opposition with the psychological intuition of time (impossible to recover because there is no psychology, at least not how we understand that concept today). However, for social phenomena, movement is associated with teleology and the idea of destiny imposed by Greek tragedy and the historical narrative. The mythical cosmogony and later on, the ancient cosmology established the idea of organizing and able to unify the principle of existence, the ultimate one concerning the diversity of the world, capable of being material, unique or multiple, even ideal. The problem of the intuition of time, discussed even today, was whether it could be established based on a natural determinism derived from physical movement or is just a form introduced by an ideal nature, either objective or subjective. The ancient patterns have imposed a circular temporality resulting from following the periodicity of the outside nature or that of the cosmic cycles. Time exists in relation to eternity, but this relation is also built in a circular way.

Time experienced as destiny:
the psychology of becoming...

We have chosen the concept of *destiny,* understood in its special sense given by Rădulescu-Motru in his philosophical system (the energetic personalism), to be able to follow the configuration of a notion of historical time because it completes his personalist dimension with a temporal one,

---

[22] Constantin Rădulescu-Motru, *Opere alese, Timp şi destin* (Selected Works, Time and Destiny), edition supervised by Gh. Vlăduşescu, Alexandru Boboc, Sabin Totu (Bucharest: Publishing of the Romanian Academy, 2006), pp. 128 – 129.

pertaining to the becoming of self and also to the social becoming. The author states right from the beginning that destiny (representing here the experienced time of the active human, socially and culturally integrated) is not a contraposition of the scientific or philosophical time, rational and abstract.

> For us, there is only one real-time, the experienced one, and we call it destiny; nowadays, the concept of time gets understood as a chronometer. This one is just a measurement instrument for periodical movements that lay above the experienced time due to their characteristic of uniform repetitions, just to record themselves on equal distances in space. The facts of life, however, bear inside the experienced time as a constituent factor. That lived time gives them uniqueness and reality.[23]

Motru's intention is a critique of the concept of time – which he succeeds in doing – but he does not insist on approaching the almost entire issue of history, which is anyhow confronted in most of his works.[24] Instead, he is

---

[23] Ibid., p. 107.

[24] Here is a chronological list of his main works in which he fulfils his social historical and phychological ideas, organized under its own system of interpretation, the energetic personalism: *Ştiinţa şi energia. Introducere* (Science and Energy. Introduction), Bucharest, The Institute of Graphic Arts „Carol Göbl", 1902, 103 p. (second edition, 1906; third edition in *Studii filosofice*, I, 1907); *Cultura română şi politicianismul* (Romanian Culture and Political Behaviour), Bucharest, Socec, 1904, VII + 192 p. (second edition, 1910; reprinted in 1984, 1995, 1998); *Puterea sufletească* (The Power of the Soul), Bucharest, *Studii filosofice* (Philosophical Studies), III, Bucharest 1908, XV – 245 p. (final edition, Casa Şcoalelor, 1930, XV + 416); *Elemente de metafizică. Principalele probleme ale filosofiei contemporane pe înţelesul tuturor* (Metaphysics Elements. The Main Contemporary Philosophical Problems explained for all), Bucharest, D. C. Ionescu Printing House, 1912, 295 p.; *Ţărănismul. Un suflet şi o politică* (Peasantry. One soul, one politics), Bucharest, National Culture 1924, 61 p.; *Personalismul energetic* (Energetic Personalism), Bucharest, Casa Şcoalelor Publishing, 1927, 272 p.; *Elemente de metafizică. Pe baza filosofiei kantiene* (Metaphysics Elements. Based on Kant's Philosophy), final edition, Casa Şcoalelor Publishing, 1928, 227 p. (reprinted in 1984, 1997, 2005); *Vocaţia. Factor hotărâtor în cultura popoarelor* (Vocation. Decisive Factor in the Culture of Mases), Casa Şcoalelor Publishing, 1932, 151 p. (final edition, 1935, 151 p.; reprinted in 1984, 1997, 2006); *Românismul. Catehismul unei noi spiritualităţi* (The Romanian Character. The Catechism of a New Spirituality), Bucharest, The Foundation for Literature and Art „Regele Carol al II-lea", 1936, 215 p. (2nd edition revised, 1939; reed., 1992); *Psihologia poporului român* (The Psychology of the Romanian People), Bucharest, The Romanian Philosophy Society, 1937, 29 p. (reprinted in 1998, 1999); *Timp şi destin* (Time and Destiny), Bucharest, The Foundation for Literature and Art, 1940, 254 p. (German version: *Zeit und Schicksall,* Jena, Leipzig, Verlag von W. Gronan, 1943, X + 190 p., Bucharest,

mainly preoccupied with the intuition of time. This subject is of capital importance in the history of culture. It originates from the consciousness of self, not the reflexive one, which will emerge later as a consequence of cultural becoming, but of the profound emotive self, 'the creator of attitudes, used by man to anticipate the instigations of the exterior when instinct is lacking.' [25] Thus, an intuition of temporality as destiny was released right on the edge between emotion and reflection, into the remote history of mankind and the complexity of subjective experiences. Thanks to our need to anticipate becoming in the middle of complex events with an unclearly separated subject from the object, time got experienced at a different intensity. The later forms of time, the reflexive ones, originate from this primitive intuition of the irreversible passing of time. Therefore, the future and the past were reduced to an intense experience of the present, so they represented both a threat and a challenge to control them. That is how mysticism, art, magic and the mythological order appeared.

> Today's man, armed with a technique of culture, looks confident towards the future and sometimes with pride back into the past. Primitive man had other conditions. For him, the future was a terrifying unknown, and the past a grave of destroyed things. From him, time is like a destructive tooth. Saturn, the god of time, was portrayed as a monster devouring his children. Due to this powerful mix of subjectivism, the intuition of time originated from a subjective mosaic, certainly different from the homogeneous consistent intuition of today's scientists. To reach the last one, the human consciousness had to go through a long period of preparation.[26]

It is important to point out this stage of primitive consciousness because it is the origin of the primordial chronotropy. It organizes the different forms of the intuition of time on the level of subjective consciousness, forms out of which the reflexive reasoning consciousness will, later on, draw the sometimes-contradictory aspects of the concept of time. The abstract notion

Paideia, Vorwort, van Al. Boboc); *Etnicul românesc.Comunitate de origine, limbă și destin* (The Romanian Ethnicity. Community of origin, language and destiny), Bucharest, Casa Școalelor Publishing, 1942, 134 p. (reprinted in 1996, 1998, 1999); *Morala personalismului energetic* (The Moral of Energetic Personalism), Bucharest, Monitorul Oficial al Imprimeriilor Statului, 1946, 33 p. *(Analele Academiei Române, Memoriile Secțiunii Literare - The Annals of the Romanian Academy, Memoires of the Literary Section*, IIIrd Series, Tom., XV, Mem. 1).

[25] C. Rădulescu-Motru, *Opere alese, Timp și destin* (Selected Works, Time and Destiny), 2006, p. 167.

[26] Ibid., p. 168.

of chronology has remained sovereign. It is necessary foremost to science and lays over the original intuition.

> The mystical anticipation of becoming is the premonition of destiny. Within this premonition, the sensitive self has the intuition of the Universe order; he anticipates this order based on an inner rapport of anthropomorphic motivation, not as some relations constantly quantitative like the modern scientist sees it today. In his premonition, the changes from the outside world and man's life both flow in the same direction, as a whole; this flow never comes back to itself. Destiny ushers the atonement of damnation or the achievement of a vocation, but not as precautions justified by experience, therefore dependent on certain conditions, but *as unyielding verdicts* (our emphasis, M. P.).[27]

The above-mentioned phrase needs emphasizing because we believe it has a special significance, not just to understand the concept of Rădulescu-Motru, but also to understand the concept of time in general, as well as becoming within the history of culture. Time generates, but it also punishes. It fulfils a certain course, but it cannot get out of the way of those individualities or singularities that cannot fulfil their destiny. Time replenishes the being and protects it from the tendencies that might disintegrate it. There are not only good strings within a Gordian knot but also unfulfilled meanings that might unravel. Above all that, ever since Antiquity, any idea on time meant to fulfil a sentence, a verdict, and to reconcile existence with the being, which, under the dynamic influence of becoming looks for itself and tries to prevent a fall into an eternal swirl of new meanings or fatal decisions. Plato's time fulfils in a circular way the eternity of the Being, sustained by the dialectics of thought, which knows self-becoming. Kantian time is once again a sentence of the unified consciousness, which the metaphysical tendencies were trying to disintegrate and therefore, the need for unity turned into a transcendental circle of consciousness in general together with the rigorous schematic of categories. Kantianism itself is a strong option to constrain the being into *existing* in the bright area of Reason, where the senses cannot account for or understand the being of things, just an approximation of them (also subjective). If temporality originated in experience, which constantly becomes, then the consciousness would try in vain to reduce it to a concept, give reality a temporary verdict and build a rational temporality.

> If, therefore, we say: The senses represent objects to us as they appear, but the understanding, as they are, then the latter is not to be taken in a

---

[27] Ibid., p. 169.

transcendental but in a merely empirical way, signifying, namely, how they must be represented as objects of experience, in the thoroughgoing connection of appearances, and not how they might be outside of the relation to possible experience and consequently to sense in general, thus as objects of pure understanding. For this will always remain unknown to us, so it even remains unknown whether such a transcendental (extraordinary) cognition is possible at all, at least as one that stands under our customary categories. With us, understanding and sensibility can determine an object only in combination. If we separate them we have intuitions without concepts or concepts without intuitions, but in either case, representations that we cannot relate to any determinate object.[28]

Apriorism is thus a rational verdict (necessary), just like Bergson's intuitionism is a mandatory verdict because, at least concerning judgements relative to time, some aspects (which have proven to be essential) of reality as becoming have remained unexplained. For example, the genesis of the intuition of time is called duration by Bergson. However, understanding that time is historical in itself, it becomes and gets replenished, just like Motru proves. A good example is the attempt to formulate the concept of experienced time (both historical and psychological at the same time) under the name of destiny related to vocation.

For C. Rădulescu-Motru, destiny is significant to spiritual becoming and has the purpose of an 'individual law', intrinsic to the substance of the soul. Destiny defines less the individual and more the nation that the individual is a part of but only manifests through an intense experience of time on the level of individual consciousness. Described by a cause-effect relationship, movement implies the conventional abstract time, 'invented by reason to establish the recurring and uniform phenomena of nature.' We can predict natural phenomena thanks to chronological time, an invariable and irreversible constant throughout their entire existence; prediction follows the rules described by science because natural phenomena repeat themselves, but the conditions of their manifestation remain relatively constant. For the phenomena of the soul, there is no repetition. They only exist in the present moment, still being a part of a seamless manifestation, a reasonable, even predictable whole, because their underlayer is a substance and an order we can rationally understand. If the substance of the soul was chaotic or irrational, Motru thinks there would not be any coherent phenomena possible within our spiritual, social and historical life. 'An irrational substance would be a substance outside of us, one that we will never be aware

---

[28] Immanuel Kant, *Critique of pure reason,* translated and edited by Paul Guyer, University of Pennsylvania, Allen W. Wood, Yale University (Cambridge University Press, 1998), p. 364.

of.'[29] The real, comprehensible world, either material or spiritual, is still rational. According to Motru, the most compelling argument is that of scientific advancement, which shows us, especially related to material phenomena, that there is a 'continuity in the rational making of the universe.'[30] The problem is we cannot predict spiritual or historical phenomena based on a universal law because their becoming is not isonomic (*isonomia* is a Greek concept meaning 'equality of political rights'), even if, from a physical, physiological and psychological perspective, the individual is a part of nature and must obey its general laws.

> From a spiritual perspective, we have the same vortex of elements forming after laws identical to those of human beings in general. *The singular originality establishes its meaning of life through the individual man* (s. n., M. P.), and consists of those moments filled with his present, the moments when he lives his destiny. In those moments, the human being gets to be unique in its way. It is the only situation in which the individuality of the human being cannot be replaced. [31]

As an individual being, man experiences the moment subjectively, and this subjectivity manifests in the present, for both his previous life (which from a historical and psychological perspective can be considered *a given*) and the anticipation of its historical passing. We can predict the conditions of its organic and psychological nature, but never with the same precision in any successive moment of its historical existence. According to Motru, this is precisely what Emil Du Bois-Reymond was trying to illustrate when he was discussing the possibility of creating an identical copy of Caesar from a psycho-physical perspective. Even if we could make such a copy (genetics and biophysics say it is possible), is it also possible to recreate the same historical conditions from when the original Caesar lived before the Rubicon? That could only be possible if we were also able to recreate the same conditions of life from the year 49 BC (individual, meaning psychological and physical, but also social and even cosmic), which would mean a 'comeback into the way life works, *eine ewige Wiederkunft* as Fr. Nietzsche wanted because only this kind of comeback would bring identity between our copy and Caesar and result in two people having the same destiny!' [32]

---

[29] C. Rădulescu-Motru, *Opere alese, Timp și destin* (Selected Works, Time and Destiny), 2006, p. 185.

[30] Ibid.

[31] Ibid., p. 183.

[32] Ibid., p. 184.

The issue raised by Motru in *Time and Destiny* brings back into discussion psychological and historical time. The philosopher analyses in detail both their historical and methodological roots, but this does not mean he also solves the issue. According to him, destiny is based on a historical tradition that 'enjoyed' much appreciation until Christianity appeared. This religion treats this issue differently and sees its solution in a world beyond, not this one. The solution for destiny is redemption. In Greek mythology, the Moirai decided each individual's destiny ever since birth. They were able to avoid any determination because even the gods feared them. Since there will be other occasions to talk about time and destiny, according to Motru, we shall note this concept as one of the anthropological models of insertion in time.

... and the stylistic determination of cultures

We should mention at least two examples related to this aspect: the first one belonging to Blaga, from his *Historical Being* and *Horizon and Style*, and the second one to Noica from *Becoming Within Being*, but compared with Cioran and Eliade.

Blaga approaches history using the instrument of categories from the philosophy of culture, even though his reference book ends the trilogy (*The Cosmological Trylogy)* it is part of. In reality, the ontological – and historical – is an issue that cannot be separated from the epistemological due to the special metaphysic structure of its philosophical system that has the *ontology of mystery* right in the middle. We must understand stylistic fields (stylistic matrix) as fundamental in the philosophy of history; they 'design' not only the spiritual activity (conscious) or social action but also the economic, one pertaining to the individual and the community. Historical experience is firstly organised by the rational, aware categories and then 'encouraged' by a set of abysmal unconscious structures, just as much of a 'modeller' as the categories of consciousness, but in a completely different ontological way. The theory of stylistic fields developed in *The Trilogy of Culture* and *The Trilogy of Value* was established by studying the domains of culture in science, art, and metaphysics, with little emphasis on political and social history. Therefore, a new perspective on history arose to complete his philosophical system. Blaga does so in *The Historical Being*: 'The material given to us by the political history of nations to illustrate the theory (of stylistic fields – n.n., M. P.) is not less conclusive than the material gathered through the purely spiritual fields.' [33] Within historical phenomena we can differentiate between a biological,

---

[33] L. Blaga, *Fiinţa istorică*, 1977, p. 88.

purely natural determination or a geographical one and one more stylistic. Society is an exclusively exterior, a man-made structure, built together with other people to preserve the specie and itself. It is also a spiritual cosmos, a biological and cultural organism. 'Society tends towards revealing the mystery in stylistic terms because society itself is structured on concepts of stylistic categories, it overcomes nature and, compared to it, it is a phenomenon completely new.'[34] As a historical being and an integral part of a social organism, man lives its time as a natural biological being that will never be able to accomplish itself as man, unless under the occurrence of the unconscious stylistic structures of the cultural phenomenon. There is a sort of an exterior 'order', a determinism assumed by need (for example, the attempts to 'civilise' and bring culture using foreign political intervention like those from Phanariot or later on, communism), a determinism specific to humans, an 'order' inside the temptations and boundaries of life, a cosmologic order, a law of nature with cosmic significance, passed on and kept from generation to generation[35] in the works of both Ovidiu Papadima and Constantin Noica.

---

[34] Ibid., p. 82.

[35] The work of Ovidiu Papadima, *O viziune românească a lumii* (A Romanian View of the World), Bucharest, 1941, uses the hermeneutics of Romanian pronunciation applied to folkloric creation. In a particular perspective it resonates with Mircea Vulcănescu's results from his research called *Dimensiunea românească a existenței* (The Romanian Dimension of the Being)*.* The concepts he analyses, *order* and *orderliness*, are part of a greater perspective of the Romanians on the social and cosmologic order, as well as a more narrow one on the spiritual. The latter concept allowed Noica to write one of his cycles of uttering Romanian philosophy. Alexandru Surdu wrote on Papadima's contribution towards appreciating a new 'dimension' of popular ontology in his book *Comentarii la rostirea filosofică însoțite de câteva gânduri despre Constantin Noica* (Comments on the philosophical uttering together with some thoughts on Constantin Noica), the chapter called *Ovidiu Papadima despre „rânduială* (Ovidiu Papadima on 'orderliness'), Brașov, Kron-Art Publishing, 2009). 'Orderliness is not just a simple order or the official guardian of order and discipline. Șăineanu translates it with *Ordnung* and *Fügung*, both connected to discipline, which proves that Papadima was right to consider orderliness without Western correspondence. […] Orderliness is not some order "established and guarded by humans". It is a law of nature, and it has a cosmic significance. Humans do not create nor guard it, but try to respect it anywhere and anytime, as long as they are aware and know it." (Al. Surdu, *Comentarii la rostirea filosofică însoțite de câteva gânduri despre Constantin Noica*, p. 68).   The concept directs us towards an immanent ontic structure, with its roots in prehistory and meanings that partially fit the ontology of the traditional Romanian village from Blaga's *Historical Being* while referencing "the world's order", a synonym for humans with god's wisdom. "The connection of the Romanian peasant with his environment gets accomplished by respecting the ordinance fitted to his *nature*. Disrespecting the ordinance, even unintentional, out of

There is a 'game' of categories and determinisms in this intertwining of historical time with the natural one (or the cultural models with the temporal ones), which forces man to understand the dialectics and the logic of the stylistic matrix. Approaching this from Spengler's perspective, cultures have a longer or a shorter curve of evolution: first, they are born, then they reach the peak, afterwards, they start declining, and finally, they die. But for Blaga, culture fits into its horizon in which temporality gets articulated by the major changes of the dynamic of the historical phenomenon, identified as such in the major economic, social or political events and divided into periods according to not only to the theoretical principles but also to the laws specific to the stages or the long periods of history. Besides the essential divisions, done according to political, economic and cultural criteria, history also has major structures, divided in a classical way between the two ages: prehistory and accurate history. Prehistory has its metaphysical structures, and we can see its effects even in historical life, especially in those areas unaffected by civilisation, the traditional villages. Blaga believes that to understand prehistory, we must comprehend the significance of the concepts he introduced in *Geneza metaforei şi sensul (The Genesis of the Metaphor and The Meaning*, Bucharest, 1937): the minor culture and the major culture. For now, we are interested in the minor ones, specifically their creative spontaneity, the refusal of prediction and the fact that they do not work as a concept of recurrence, even though there are values that we need to work with presumed by a model of the cosmological time.

> The minor culture keeps man closer to nature while the major one pushes him away and alienates him from Nature's order.' [36] In return, the major culture deliberately sets out to defeat time; it exists in permanent tension with its existential space and wants to assert itself at any cost. That causes it to be exposed to all the progressive and evolutionary temptations while at the same time being able to integrate exterior forms and contents that wish to synchronize with it. In general, major cultures do not reckon on duration without the risk – regularly pointed out – of overloading with models and contradicting hierarchies of values. They get exposed to other dangers, including 'catastrophe and death'. The differences between the temporal and the evolutionary patterns do not necessarily also involve differences in value, even though there is almost a rule that the owners of a major culture 'look at the minor ones over their shoulder. [37]

---

ignorance, could lead to harmful events, narrated in all sorts of tales" (Ibid., pp. 70 – 71).

[36] L. Blaga, *Fiinţa istorică*, 1977, p. 50.

[37] Ibid.

Our point of interest for now, in the dialectics of both models, is that there is also a secondary dialectics of the temporal form thinkers are just considering, connected to the distinction between prehistory and the proper history. Most historians, anthropologists and philosophers of culture assign prehistory the status of a cultural matrix, the origin and source of all historical cultures. Blaga mentions Vico, Schelling and L. Klages because they got to analyse the spiritual values of prehistory or history and the distinction between the temporal patterns that belong to each of these ages. Vico was among the first to mention the notion of historical and cultural cycles, paying attention to the beginning age (childhood) of humanity. According to Schelling, there are major differences between those two related to nature and the dynamics of the actions of conscience. Prehistoric time coincides with a crisis of the human conscience, one extremely creative from a spiritual perspective, that gave birth to myths and the division of humanity into nations. One cannot establish historical time before the peoples assert themselves as distinctive spatial and temporal entities. A quality of these prehistoric cultures is that there is a 'monumental vision' in the art that has emerged inside of them (Egyptian architecture, the Persian etc.) that could qualify those cultures as major ones, to quote Schelling. More important than this is that, from the perspective of the spirit, in prehistory, the mythological creation was similar to the 'divine revelation' of historical time.

> Mythology would be *the analogue* of divine revelation. Mythology exists thanks to a conscience process fuelled by divine inspirations. This is the only way we can understand the truly exceptional products of that *chronos àdilos* or any other from prehistoric time.'[38]

Consequently, psychological time is more complex than the physiological time, which is also superior to chemical and biochemical processes. However, this 'progression' is relative from the perspective of complexity, and this is proven by the very complicated temporal relations on a microphysical level or that of quantum physics.

Time gains new meaning if we start in reverse, from the processes of living towards organising social and historical life. The spatial and temporal structures become more complex as we go deeper into interplanetary space or as we overcome the depth of the cosmos. The same happens if we investigate in the opposite direction, towards the microscopic area of life or the macroscopic one, of geological and biological systems etc. Seen while becoming, the world becomes more diverse, its space-time relations bind

---

[38] Ibid., p. 53.

and unbind so that the cosmos and the microcosm start revealing to us like islands on a permanently active archipelago. Space and time intertwine. Time itself is no longer a one-lineal constant, even though the law of causality and general determinism does not seem to invalidate this reality. If we look at reality from the perspective of temporality, the element that stands out in the light of this determinism is *connectivity*, which is not just a relative constant to the order of space, but also a dynamic reality, mainly temporal: time binds, intertwines elements and creates a network of events with general and individual meanings. The reflex of this complex reality observed from a diachronic perspective is the historical 'craving' of philosophy and modern epistemology. As a matter of fact, time has become an obsession (not just for historians and philosophers) extensively exploited, especially in modern times. History, together with its apparent irrational becoming, has puzzled the spirit, and it is impossible to have been less intriguing than the desire for universality and stability proper to the ancient Greek spirit.

References

Blaga, Lucian. 1977. *Fiinţa istorică* (The Historical Being), supervised edition, notes and preface by Tudor Cătineanu. Cluj-Napoca: Dacia Publishing.

Eliade, Mircea. 1959. *The Myth of The Eternal Return,* translated from French by Willard R. Trask. New York: Harper&Brathers Publishers.

Eliade, Mircea. 1959. *Sacred and The Profane. The Nature of Religion*, translated from French by Willard R. Trask. New York: Harcourt, Brace&World, Inc.

Iorga, Nicolae. 1944. *Permananţele istoriei* (The Permanences of History), speech held at The International History Congress in Zürich, september, 1938, in *Generalităţi cu privire la studiile istorice* (General ideas on historical studies), 3rd edition. Bucharest: The Institute of Universal History „N. Iorga".

Iorga, Nicolae. 1987. *Evoluţia ideii de libertate* (The Evolution of the Idea of Freedom), supervised edition, introductive study and notes by Ilie Bădescu. Bucharest: Meridiane Publishing.

Kant, Immanuel. 1998. *Critique of pure reason,* translated and edited by Paul Guyer, University of Pensylvania, Allen W. Wood, Yale University. Cambridge University Press.

Pârvan, Vasile. 2006. *Scrieri alese, Studii şi eseuri, III. Despre ritmul istoric,* (Selected Works, Studies and Essays, III. On the Historical rhythm), opening lesson from the lecture on *Istoria religiunilor* (The

History of Religions)*, held during the summer semester MCMXX at the University of Bucharest, read on the 4th of February MCMXX), introduction and notes by Alexandru Zub, preface (for the princeps edition) by Radu Vulpe. Bucharest: Publishing of the Romanian Academy.

Plato. 1997. *Timaeos*, translated by Donald J. Zeyl, in *idem, Complete Works,* edited, with Introduction and Notes, by John M. Cooper, associate editor D.S. Hutchinson. Indianapolis/Cambridge: Hacket Publishing Company.

Rădulescu-Motru, Constantin. 2006. *Opere alese, Timp şi destin* (Selected Works, Time and Destiny), edition supervised by Gh. Vlăduşescu, Alexandru Boboc, Sabin Totu. Bucharest: Publishing of the Romanian Academy.

Surdu, Alexandru. 2009. *Comentarii la rostirea filosofică însoţite de câteva gânduri despre Constantin Noica* (Comments on the philosophical uttering together with some thoughts on Constantin Noica), the chapter called *Ovidiu Papadima despre „rânduială"* (Ovidiu Papadima on 'orderliness'). Braşov: Kron-Art Publishing.

Vulcănescu, Mircea. 1991. *Dimensiunea românească a existenţei* (The Romanian Dimension of Existence), edition supervised by Marin Diaconu. Bucharest: Publishing of Fundaţiei Culturale Române.

CHAPTER II

EXPERIENCE AND HISTORICAL FACT

Experience and history

The supporting point of history is the reality of the experienced fact, individualized in time and, thus, elevated to have a social significance. The memory of the action (the social collective memory) offers the document extra historical credibility. If this were not a more significant event than just an accident in the course of life, equal to any other and without any major social or individual consequences, it would not become a historical fact. The friendship between Peter the Great and Dimitrie Cantemir is an event in their biography as individuals but also plays a part in the destiny of a collectivity, as it deviates the normal historical course of events and fundamentally reconfigures their social, political, economic and cultural journey through life. This friendship becomes a historical fact that exceeds the biography of the individuals because it can change the biography of a nation.

Historical experience is not a concept meant to ease the ascension of the historical to the degree of fact. It is tightly connected to the fact but does not make it easier to handle, because fact itself is retractile and hides its social essence (cultural) and significance inside time. Starting from a concept we have already tried to metaphorically sketch, the present time within the past,[1] where the historical present (of the narrator) rebuilds in a continuous change of perspective the diachronic fact in search for *the present time* of the past *action*, we get to a point where experience suddenly becomes a relation between two temporal realities, both looking for their own cultural identity. Looking at it from this perspective, history proceeds along with us; our present and the past present become like two mirrors impossible to move

---

[1] Mihai Popa, *Individul – „prizonier al istoriei"* (The Individual – „a captive of history"), in *Studii de istorie a filosofiei românești* (Studies on the History of Romanian Philosophy), vol. III, *Omagiu profesorului Alexandru Surdu* (An Homage to professor Alexandru Surdu), coordinated by Viorel Cernica, ed. Supervised by Mona Mamulea (Bucharest: Publishing House of the Romanian Academy, 2008), pp. 165–170.

due to the weight of conceptualizing a fulfilled reality given by the understandable weight (impossibility) of fact (experience). The historical pushes the present away into the past more so as it tries to reveal it to its present (the moment it writes in and for which it writes). This fact persuades us not to give up in front of the relativity of writing: 'History's matter is not stable, nor steadfast, but moving; *the present* continuously *creates a past...*' [2]

The question is whether the event we are extracting the historical experience from obtains the status of historical fact precisely when it happens (thus has a general-historical meaning right from the beginning) or is it *becoming,* as an effect of remembering throughout generations thanks to the historical direction and socio-cultural valorization done in time? In other words, is it reflected and amplified with every ulterior moment added (in both significance and value), becoming an act of experience in time, as the perspectives of future generations bring new qualities to memory (a memory which assumes the result of this becoming from the present's perspective)? To understand historical experience – of a particularly special sort and made from the same substance as any other experience from other fields – we must consider the time factor, just as we can conclude from all previously mentioned.

Historical experience requires at least two references. Firstly, there is the relation between fact and narration (recording it into collective memory) which becomes a document at a moment of more or less proximity to the event. We can call this first reference the initial source, the primordial fact that initiates the intercepting process of a historical act which will, from this moment on, transform into a historical experience. However, at first glance, this narration is man's deed – left as proof without the intention of becoming a document – but looking closer, we know this is man's deed and it has been transformed on purpose into a motive (an adapted document: a chronicle, an inscription, a monument, a literary work mistaken for a historical source) which becomes a reason for historical consideration. There is a generality margin between these two categories of confessions. In general, the first random and unintentionally processed archaeological findings for their narrative 'reason' gain an ulterior degree of generality at the other end of temporality (the time segment that stands between the time of conceiving and that of discovering and interpreting it) remaining 'silent' throughout the entire period they were 'undeciphered', and having no intention of a proof that could be carried in time. The second category of documents promotes

---

[2] Neagu Djuvara, *Există istorie adevărată? Despre „relativitatea generală" a istoriei. Eseu de epistemologie* (Is there a true history? On „the general relativity" of history. Epistemology essay), (Bucharest: Humanitas Publishing, 2008), p. 7.

right from the start a message with a historical 'reason', as they have been kept precisely with this purpose throughout generations: they leave *clues* ready to be deciphered and are constantly challenged and promoted.

Historical experience – the first approximation of reality while continuously becoming – is how history decodes the information contained by the historical document, reshaping it with instruments from the present to conserve the initial message and expose it to present consciousness as a value trapped in time.

This activity can have a double purpose: 1. To present as detached as possible some elements (always extracted from a whole they still suggest but never recompose) from a previous life; 2. To use these elements as means to recreate a historical reality inside the researcher's consciousness and of all the other participants in the historical 'reading'. We are generally supposed to assume this historical reality thanks to our historical condition of beings that pass and continuously become (historical beings). This second meaning can take up various forms as a 'literary' expression and is the one we have in mind when we attempt sketch the premises of historical experience. Of course, some diligence will always come in handy for aspects and conceptual relations that offer the possibility to capture more profound data of reality. The first sentence – an assertion with a clear significance for historical experience – was proposed by researchers preoccupied with distinguishing between lived history and described history.

This distinction is not only subtle but also obvious when the researcher needs to connect his work (narration) to the deeds of a man that has become the object of the narration: documents preserved as proof without the intention of being historical documents as such and also documents which contain the historical object as intention plus the inevitable subjectivity (extremely significant to research), built right from the moment of their 'introduction' in man's narration as the deeds of a man who is aware of his history and he proposes them to the future (historical awareness). We must relate the experience to both meanings of the fact and introduce in its sphere the two historical 'ways' we have mentioned above, history-experience and history-description. Another name for this type of history is the real-past or *Geschichte,* a term proposed by German researchers, along with *Historie,* which means written history (even though it is irrelevant to our purpose of understanding the characteristics of historical experience). Neagu Djuvara notices the artificiality of terms and their ability to interchange sometimes. Following this idea, he sees in Arthur C. Danto's work a distinction between fields that might also prove useful to our work. The American philosopher comes up with a term (and also an area for thought) for history as a relic: *History as Record,* intertwined with the other two: *History as Actuality*

(*Geschicte*, for the Germans, *Histoire* for the French) for experienced history and *Histoire*, used by the Germans for the written history, while the French use it, but without the capital letter: *histoire*.[3]

Experience and knowledge

As shown above, we believe historical experience references the written history that already got into the public conscience through discourse. Its effect becomes visible in the interpretation, the discourse and the research rather than in the historical 'empathy', in the staging of a drama that other people lived or in the recreation of the conditions of that experience. But is not written history often lost on the way precisely because its direct message, linked to the source and to experience as a fact, gets diluted? The historical fact derived from the discourse is less able to support experience because in any of its strong meanings, in any field, the experience remains alive thanks to a life-like direct connection with the reality of a deed and with history as history, but less with history-narration (the discourse).

In any discourse, in the sciences, the arts and the religious experience, experience is immediate. 'Experience is a word with legitimate potency because it shows the path of the best and certain "information". To build experience means "to learn straight from reality", to receive "first hand" knowledge, that means from a direct primordial dwelling with everything.'[4]

Historical experience is appropriated through means acknowledged mainly as being a part of an experienced act in other fields, but is it direct, at first hand? Does it connect us to the reality of history so that our relationship becomes immediate and not mediated by the raw deed? Obviously, we are far from an absolute affirmation. In general, experience is held responsible for not contributing to knowledge other than passively and immediately, which is partially true if we consider that for Aristotle and Kant too, experience sometimes has a synthetic or active role; it is a connection *bridge* between individual and general (particular and universal). It is often said that experience focuses on the particular, on what is due to change and not on the universal and necessary privilege of thinking. Reason denies the experience of its strong attributes (functions) that are able to reveal the essence or foundation of existence.

---

[3] Neagu Djuvara, *Există istorie adevărată? Despre „relativitatea generală" a istoriei. Eseu de epistemologie,* 2008, pp. 18–19.
[4] Mircea Florian, *Paradoxele experienței* (The Paradoxes of Experience), in *Experiența ca principiu de reconstrucție filosofică* (Experience as a principle of philosophical reconstruction), (Bucharest: Gramar Publishing, 2002), p. 242.

While the Parmenidean being is unique and permanent, the Heraclitean one represents becoming (an eternal alive fire), and both philosophers believe that our senses do not provide us with certainty, even if they have different reasons to believe this. For Heraclitus is 'because they represent things uniformly and unchanging; [for] Parmenides because he shows them to us as being numerous and dominated by variation.'[5] Our mistrust in the senses reaches its peak with Plato when the sensitive, linked to the particular, is yanked from the thought, the universal and the Idea, which obtains an absolute reality. We must not forget that in this process of separation between experience and thought, two new concepts emerge: one is conceptualism, which means the universal is brought from the field of real-absolute into the reality of our consciousness, which then completes the rupture of the particular from the universal inside the concept by using a generalization. The second is nominalism, which means the universal becomes name:

> There is just what we can perceive, and we only perceive individual things, d. p., this or that man, but not the universal or the notion of «humanity», just a simple collective word, therefore fiction and in no way a superior reality.[6]

The balance between experience and thinking is still somehow maintained in Aristotle because experience has the door opened towards the result of thinking even though it is a road intermediated by intelligence: from the particular sensation to the universal knowledge, there is a continuous path, possible for Aristotle, because 'sensation itself holds a universal element if reason gets together with perception.'[7]

As a result, there is also a separation between the two taking place on the thinking level (which we might say is stimulated by the Platonic influence): the first one means to passively record sensory data, while the second one, active by definition, handles the material given by perception and reaches the concept. Following a seemingly epistemological conciliation in time, between data coming from experience and the categories of thinking, Aristotle will discuss the two functions separately and sometimes consider them as absolute and generalize them. That is how thinking gets to be understood as something passive above all by John Locke and shaped by the sensorial impressions, while for Berkeley 'thinking is so active that it

---

[5] Ibid., p. 244.
[6] Ibid., *Experienţa ca principiu de reconstrucţie filosofică, (Experienţă şi matematică),* (Experience and mathematics), 2002, p. 155.
[7] Ibid., p. 245.

represents itself the object of knowledge.'[8] This issue of the rapport between the two is going to become the ground foundation in the creation of what we call epistemological anthropology. The relation between the object and the subject of knowledge cannot elude experience and a synthesis of these relations (translated hither or beyond experience – Kant's solution or through the epistemological reduction of experience to a subjective act without any connection to the existential object – Berkeley) cannot go around the epistemological traits of historical experience.

Historical experience can neither avoid the duality of the acts of consciousness, nor the relation particular-universal. If according to this historically configured decision, experience represents the field of those assertions that only have an individual (particular) connotation, then we need to ask if it is necessary or able to build awareness (its unconditioned validity). Knowledge without these two qualities (universality and necessity) does not exist. Therefore, the experience offers only a certain degree of relative generality (particular cases of past and present experience, limited in number) and a 'conditional'[9] necessity.

The unconditional residing in the results of abstractive power and their universal validity – categories, concepts – overshadow immediate particular and non-essential realities. Therefore, on this level, we also encounter a high degree (maybe the highest) of subjectivity. What experience tells us has gained over time (starting with Plato's idealist realism, or even earlier as seen before in Parmenide) the mark of subjectivity, as if this element of consciousness is an offence of the supremacy and self-security of reason. Nonetheless, through Aristotle's philosophy, experience (*topos* of the individual) can lay next to the universal; moreover, one of the philosopher's thesis asserts that universality is not separated from the individual:

> It is one of the current theses of the philosopher the one stating that there is only the individual. The universal exists solely in and through the individual. This belief was so deeply-rooted in Aristotle that we can rightfully believe he did not understand Plato's ideas beyond them being more than individual realities. [10]

---

[8] Alexandru Surdu, *Cercetări logico-filosofice* (Logico-philosophical Researches), edition supervised by Victor Emanuel Gica, Dragoş Popescu, Ovidiu Grama, (Bucharest: Technical Publishing, 2008), p. 50.

[9] Mircea Florian, *Experienţa ca principiu de reconstrucţie filosofică* (*Paradoxele experienţei), 2002*, p. 243.

[10] Constantin Noica, *Schiţă pentru istoria lui Cum e cu putinţă ceva nou* (A Sketch for the history of How is something new possible), (Bucharest: Humanitas Publishing, 1995), p. 106.

The matter of the relationship between the individual and the general is a central theme for Aristotle. We can even say that thanks to him, we are now convinced – previous philosophies were only groping around, including on the issue of the 'principle', a term coming from physics – that the individual 'dominates both physics and metaphysics'[11] while existence gains roundness and epistemological authority (using the traits of experience in physics).

His philosophy gives us reasons to attach experience to the faculties of consciousness that connect us to the universal, but we cannot proclaim the situation as semi-pervading. On the contrary, connecting experience to the universal is an exception, while the rule is to mistrust the first. The innate weaknesses of experience were also previously a reason for conflict between the advocates of rationalism, who trusted Plato to wear the laurels of limitless authority, and those of sensationalism, which will assert itself as a direction later on, in the modern era (empiricism).

Experience gains an intimate structure when it relates to the subject in any field. At the same time, a dose of uncertainty also gets inserted. The witness of this uncertainty is the reason. And in connection to experience, reason represents the witness that firstly defies this historic pact between the time of subjectivity referencing the sensitive deed and the time of subjectivity referencing the ideal deed removed from history. Platonic realism serves this purpose best. The epistemological treatment that separates experience from the epistemic subject and its intimate purpose linked to the universal (which is knowledge) is, paradoxically, the same treatment that strives to rehabilitate it in connection to the direct reference to the deed. This reference – an outdated historical doctrine that many embraced because it is associated with sensuality and scepticism – will gradually bring experience the renewed strengths of subjectivity, which strives to keep Platonism, realism and modern nominalism in equilibrium. Such an attitude would have been inconceivable in Platonism because it had to maintain reason within the boundaries of the universal.

> Plato offers the formula, constantly reused, against scepticism. He proves wrong the sensorial relativism of sophists and denies sensation its quality of knowledge (*episteme*) because it references becoming (*Theaitetos*), saving it only for the reason or the Idea that expresses the eternal or the consistency.[12]

From the perspective of historical experience, subjectivity has at least two references: one is generally humane, understood as a collective subject

---

[11] Ibid., p. 107.
[12] M. Florian, *Paradoxele experienţei,* 2002, p. 244.

and as a factor bearing the historicity of groups of people to which the individual consciousness relates (similar to historical consciousness in general). The other one is the consciousness of the reality of the historical time, object from the researcher's perspective (historian, philosopher) and subject from the perspective of the historical actor, the person contemporary with the deed.

The second reference is the historical being. Experience is in constant look for it through the reflexive bridge in which the two consciousnesses lay off the anchor, and in doing so, experience gains mainly its being (historical). This being is not just the individual of the experienced deed, but *becomes* an experienced fact for the entire community. The authority of the historical being regarding the historical consciousness and history (discipline), along with all the gained experience, leads us to believe we are getting history close, including its truth. According to Aristotle's principle – 'the being is truth because it is a cause of truth'[13] – the purpose of every science is the being it uncovers (for history, the historical being is the principle of truth revealed in past acts and experienced history but also in the history reflected by the historical subject). Without any doubt, history's truth is the historical perspective upon the being, and the being as being is the perquisite of philosophy. Of course, philosophy is above all other sciences (mathematics, medicine, physics etc.) because it is only interested in the being as being, while the others look at a predetermined field.[14]

What kind of a relationship can historical experience see from within the truth of its being have with the historical fact if its target is the experienced immediate particular deed? As we know, pure living alienates the truth of science, and living has no logic: the more real and personal an experience, the less true it is because living excludes logic or rational thinking.[15]

A nation begins to have historical experience when it has gathered throughout time, not just a set of historical systematic information and facts but mainly a particular ability to use this knowledge of past experiences to solve problems in the present and meet the future prepared. Historical experience is not just a necessity of evolution in history but also a mandatory tool towards historical progress. A nation without a database of historical documents or anything that can prove its historical experience does not exist, and it cannot be acknowledged as an identity in the universal dialogue. Science itself solves its problems in time. The truth of science also has a temporal side: from Ptolemy to Copernicus and Einstein or from

---

[13] C. Noica, *Schiță pentru istoria lui Cum e cu putință ceva nou,* 1995, p. 99.

[14] Aristotle, *Metaphysics*, translated with Introduction and Notes by C.D.C. Reeve (Indianapolis/Cambridge: Hackett Publishing Company, Inc., 2016), 1025 b.

[15] M. Florian, *Paradoxele experienței,* 2002, pp. 243–244.

Democritus and Hippocrates to Bohr, our image of the Universe has been constantly changing. The rhythm of history changes in every century. The real-time of nature becomes the logical time of man and thought. Real-time used to be the absolute chronological mark, but then man started embracing a clock with a different beat, authentic and proper to the human condition and its becoming. Man has thus left contemplation (practical natural wisdom) and has entered the time of his humane, historical nature:

> The intervention of logical time in history was called revolution; its intervention in knowing nature was called experiment; its intervention in transforming nature according to his needs was called civilization, and the intervention in man's work towards maturity was called education. Man has, therefore, always dealt with logical time. [16]

Logical time belongs to man, and it represents openness towards the being. Employing thought (authentic being), the time of this thinking and its irreversible passing together with becoming (its logic), they all become humane. History has no meaning unless it rises above history as experience (knowledge) of the past, gaining significance for the future. In this particular spot of becoming, Noica discovers a sense of history that brings it to philosophy because just like philosophy, history does not have to represent escape or the search for a reality expressed in the past, but rather a reality authentically humane, able to *express itself from* the past. Above real-time, frozen inside things and above the uttering time, which accounts for things by questioning reality in the presence of thought (a becoming pendant within consciousness), the time of logical becoming represents the time of man against nature or the becoming within being. Philosophy considers becoming the theme of expressing the being – the Aristotelian theme of being as being - 'the new object', which is also the forever one.

> But what does this becoming conjure after all, if not the biggest issue of ancient philosophy, transformed, or the problem of the *perennial* theme which leads to being? Are we today, through our awareness of the historical becoming, not closer than we ever were through theology or science to the *pure* form of philosophy?' [17]

Historical experience is thus a connecting element for the raw deed – particular, linked to the time and space always alienated by the subject that knows it and it is also limited by its historicity – to be able to get a historical

---

[16] Constantin Noica, *Trei introduceri la devenire întru ființă* (Three Introductions for Becoming Within Being), (Bucharest: Univers Publishing, 1984), p. 128.
[17] Ibid., pp. 61–62.

meaning; the individual deed becomes a document, an occasion to historically reflect and a link between the past and the future through the present of the epistemic subject. The historical fact would not become what it is (a deed of history which contains a necessary and generally valid truth, but not a contingency) unless the experience of the past were an occasion to modify the experience of the present. Within this relation (with a profound *methodological* trait), the true concept of the relation between experience and historical deed can be expressed: history is significant for our present just as an experience has had value for *that* present.

Dialectics and history. Historical experience – a type of spiritual communion done in time

Entering the time of history contained inside the notion of historical experience is possible. The real possibility we get from knowing history (the historical being) comes from understanding historical experience as a way to reach communion in time: it is the purpose of any knowledge, the original purpose of Plato's dialectics. We have grown apart from it due to modern science, which reifies and brings excessive logic into the reality we wish to get closer to through knowledge. Truth cannot be alienated from man, as they are a whole: we obtain it through dialogue and communion. History takes part in the being of truth, while the becoming of a historical deed (evidence that lasts) gives meaning to time and transforms it into a time of *logos* (the uttering or logic time in Noica).

Historical experience is a vague concept in Greek philosophy. If we insist to find it, we do not need to look further than Plato to discover an argument for this modern statement (Hegel, Vico, Toynbee, Collingwood) about the relation between becoming (temporality) and self-awareness. The law of the Universe – extendedly discussed in *Timaeus*[18] – maintains a fair account between becoming (established at the same time as temporality, a medium and reason for turmoil) and the pre-established order, but no less tired by the 'higher' becoming of dialectics:

> The god wanted everything to be good and nothing to be bad so far as that was possible, and so he took over all that was visible – not at rest but in discordant and disorderly motion – and brought it from a state of disorder to

---

[18] Plato, *Timaeos*, in *idem, Coplete Works,* edited, with Introduction and Notes, by John M. Cooper, associate editor D.S. Hutchinson (Indianapolis/Cambridge: Hacket Publishing Company, 1997), pp. 1224–1291.

one of order, because he believed that order was in every way better than a disorder. [19]

We must not forget that *Timaeus* brings into the dialogue the notion of becoming to postulate that the world identical to itself, which is the ground for the harmony of the universal model (of ideas), is contrary to history because the latter degrades the notion. The model is untouchable; what is identical to itself is a source of perfection for the historical world, and time itself is a copy of eternity. But we can distance ourselves from the pre-established harmony through becoming; the becoming corrupts the law; the becoming corrupts the law.

> So whenever the craftsman looks at what is always changeless and, using a thing of that kind as his model, reproduces its form and character, then, of necessity, all that he so completes is beautiful. But were he to look at a thing that has come to be and use as his model something that has been begotten, his work will lack beauty. [20]

In its broadest sense, experience designates direct contact with reality, the source and the initial task we start from to build the concept. *Experientia* (*experiri*) gets us closer to reality in the most direct way, through sensations. We can broadly include historical experience as life experience and synthesis of life – through multiple failures and their gradual elimination in time. Within the theory of knowledge, the first meaning (the first one used when we need to consider the epistemological component) contributes to the activation of experience and also to the limitation of the knowledge's validity (the general law) as a criterion dedicated to this and strengthen by experiment. Modern science has outbid the experiment, thus resulting in modern-day physics in the experiment's inability to be constructed without theoretical means and to become inconclusive as actual evidence in the classical sense.

Taking over the first meaning of experience, used mainly in the natural sciences, leads to dualism. Any interpretation of a fact exists in terms of this reality to which we add a drop of generality (the concept). But, by limiting the experience to the particular and minimizing its role in shaping consciousness through compensation, we end up giving more credit to the concept, as far as cutting any support in the fact (rationalism). We notice the same thing in history, maybe even more so, where experience is not direct (we do not have direct access to the historical fact of life) but temporal and intermediated by confessions (documents). The distinction between the

---

[19] Ibid., p. 1236 (30 a).
[20] Ibid., pp. 1234–1235 (28 a-b).

individual and the particular is a necessary abstraction for science, just like Collingwood noticed, but does not require generalization because knowledge is a complex act, while the pure particular and the pure universal are nothing but false abstractions. [21]

If we were to diminish the epistemic presence of the individual within the construction of the concept, it would be like amputating the pivotal root of consciousness, meaning the reality and the authority of the fact meant to reveal to us. We cannot put into shade the individual traits, particularly in attaining historical knowledge. Using experience, we can check the generalities formulated through successive abstractions within the individual. Science in general and history in particular verify the stability of individual qualities, elevating them in successive degrees until they transform their quality into a permanence, a category of existence.[22] Knowing the phenomena is done through the individual, repeatedly and continuously, without any failure. The permanence of the universe gives a continuity that is also reflected in individual deeds. The fact that we can elevate traits from the individual level (induction) to the level of concept gives us confidence in our capacity to appropriate from temporality (change) those elements that can last from reality.

> For knowledge seems to be something permanent and hard to change if one has even a moderate grasp of a branch of knowledge unless a great change is brought about by illness or some other such thing. So also a virtue; justice, temperance, and the rest seem not easily changed. [23]

Change is a concept which confuses the spirit. It belongs to temporality, and it is development, becoming through temporality, able to inoculate experience – this way we have a 'steady' concept, strictly delimitated by the generality constantly building our consciousness – with its historical dimension.

All the other forms of experience – artistic, religious and even within the experiment – also have a temporal element, but it is not as visible as the historical experience.

---

[21] See Sergiu Bălan, *Între istorie și filosofie. Sistemul lui R. G. Collingwood* (Between history and philosophy. The system of R. G. Collingwood), (Bucharest: Publishing of the Romanian Academy, 2009), pp. 88–89.

[22] Aristotle, *Categories and De Interpretatione*, translated with Notes by J.L. Ackrill, Clarendon Aristotle Series, general editors J.L. Ackrill and Lindsay Judson (New York: Oxford University Press, 1963), pp. 24–31 (8b–11a).

[23] Ibid., p. 24 (8 b).

Historical experience – a type of *historical community*

Several doses of mistrust have been inoculated into the experience as it was always seen as this incompatible opponent of the law's universal, towards which science tends to go. We might say that beyond empiricism, or maybe thanks to it, the modern disease of historicism – false disease – would not be able to corrupt history or experience, but it will make them stronger. Kant himself is unable to see the possibility of knowledge given strictly by the categories of thought because his premise states that there is a difference between thinking and knowing an object.[24] The possibility of the consciousness existing (its transcendental dimension) does not take away the possibility of the object forming intuitively.

> Now all intuition that is possible for us is sensible (Aesthetic), thus for us thinking of an object in general through a pure concept of the understanding can become cognition only insofar as this concept is related to objects of the senses. [25]

Apriorism is just a focus on thinking that does not shed a dense shadow over the deeds of experience. The scholastic distinction between *a posteriori* and *a priori* is used not so much to negate the positive (and beneficial) rapport between experience and thinking, but mainly to emphasize the two different ways of approaching reality. The right thing to do is place them in a receding relationship, just like Florian did. Otherwise, we will always stumble upon the dualism experience/reason. [26] Neither of them will ever be on trial, made to testify against the other. By offering mutual support, they can justify their results together: knowing the fact implies they agree and work together to obtain a common goal and not irrevocably take over a process of consciousness by one of them. Therefore, the conclusion we can draw from apriorism is not an accuse we bring experience but a recognition of it:

> The pure concepts of the understanding, consequently, even if they are applied to apriori intuitions (as in mathematics), provide cognition only insofar as these a priori intuitions, and using them also the concepts of the understanding, can be applied to empirical intuitions. Consequently, the

---

[24] Immanuel Kant, *Critique of pure reason,* translated and edited by Paul Guyer, University of Pennsylvania, Allen W. Wood, Yale University (Cambridge University Press, 1998), p. 254.

[25] Ibid.

[26] Mircea Florian, *Recesivitatea ca structură a lumii* (Retraction as structure of the world), vol. I (Bucharest: Publishing of Pro Foundation, 2003), p. 253.

categories do not afford us cognition of things employing intuition except through their possible application to empirical intuition, i.e., they serve only for the possibility of empirical cognition. [27]

The visible tendency while making a logical and historical analysis of experience is to pair it up with knowledge, although its forms, mainly the three we have already observed – historical, religious and artistic experience – urge us to reflect on another component, no less important than the others: the spiritual communion. The moment we receive the Eucharist (gr. *eukharistia* < *kharis*, favour, grace), we reach the essence of this connection, preserved in most religions = communion, oblation, sacrament, complete engagement in the original creation (attained symbolically through ritualistic behaviour or anthropologic or sociologic interpretations) and returning to the principle, the god. This tendency also exists in the artistic experience, but not the same. The artistic experience implies a communion that manifests in two directions: on one hand, there is the experience of the artist *inside* the investigated object which is also the target of creation. On the other hand, there is the contribution of the art recipient, who helps himself from the drama or joy expressed by the artistic creator. Both experiences oppose the modern concept of experiment connected to execution, innovation and mechanical reproduction. All these elements considered part of the experimental technique *invade* the original reality and insert at least one allogeneic factor that alienates the subject from an uncontaminated source of truism or a direct experience.

Historical experience invades, at least through its original intentions, the idea of invasive knowledge. Its original idea is *communion.* The derived meanings of this term (fr. *communion*, lat. *communio*) come down to one, also present in *the Eucharist,* and implies an intense long-lasting experience, a union in which all participants take part willingly. Another meaning leads to displaying this experience and then passing it on to others through *communication:* creating connections between shared ideas.

Moreover, communion does not simply mean putting things (goods) in common. It means agreeing spiritually, and it has two significances: first, the original one means faith, complete and unconditionally shared. The second meaning refers to accepting an idea and then passing it from one person to another, not as an experience, but more as an elevation towards concept through dialogue – the Platonic dialectics.

In Hegel, however, conjugated with time or the historic becoming, dialectics might lose its initial meaning. Historical logic can be approached faster by a 'tetradic' dialectics (notion used by Noica or T. Vianu) when we

---

[27] Immanuel Kant, *Critique of pure reason*, 1998, pp. 254–255.

consider becoming (and history) within the circularity it fulfils (becoming within being, in Noica's case), the supreme genera of Plato (being, movement, the identical, the different), or a pentadic dialectics that can offer an open structure, similar to the social or cultural becoming. Pitagora's followers reserved the pentadic structures for life in general, but also for

> the most profound structures of matter, considered of a geometrical nature (the five perfect shapes), as well as the artistic fields (music, architecture, sculpture, and painting have valid pentadic representations even today that make for the essential elements in the penta-morphosis of art).[28]

Temporal Closeness – communicating (confessing) a historical reality

The paradox of historical knowledge emerges when it expresses the condition of the historical fact – which is individual, but it also contains a universal revealed in time through historical consciousness. The person trying to know uses the criteria of his time to reach a reality he does not have direct access to. No knowledge is straight, not even that from natural sciences, because a temporal barrier exists in every type. If we consider the physical reality on a macro or a micro level, there is always a temporal gap between the subject and the object. By analysing the structures from beyond our solar system, we see that this gap exceeds the temporal dimension of human culture in size. However, our object of study here is the relation fact-confession, not fact-object. For this idea of historical communion done *in time*, the circumstance of confession (a witness in time for the other, who will understand me, get into my time and get me into his time as well, by default; he will confess me) represents precisely the connection between two entities able to identify each other in time: the one knowing becomes himself known. We can discuss here the reversibility of historical time and the migration of historical fact between two historical realities that merge into one: historical knowledge. If we ignore this possibility provoked mainly by historical experience (it also contains it), then historical knowledge will be corrupted in its purpose – bringing together two worlds divided by time. The underlying indecision of the knowledge-historical existence relation leads to mistrust in the historical being's ability to know itself. The becoming reality exists just by becoming.

---

[28] Alexandru Surdu, *Ipostazele dialecticii* (Aspects of dialectics), in *Cercetări logico-filosofice* (Logical and philosophical researches), (Bucharest: Tehnică Publishing, 2008), p. 86.

But we've not only shown that *those which are not* are. We've also caused what turns out to be the form of *that which is not* to appear. Since we showed that the nature of *the different* exists, chopped up among all beings in relation to each other, we dared to say that *that which is not* real is just this, namely, each part of the nature of the different that's set over against *that which is*. [29]

The historical fact becomes (it is not fixed) immobile in an extinct world: through its becoming, it confesses precisely about the world that created it and confesses about the man.

Historical confession – how most historical sources are labelled – carries in itself the intention of communion: a curve in time, a connection (reconnection) of two entities, a spiritual communion which represents the essence of the historical being – the being passing through time and assumes it. Only you can understand me (I have got no purpose in your absence), the one that will follow me. At the same time, you, the one that understands me, have no purpose – you cannot get inside your time – if you do not confess to me. I know you because you will assimilate me (communicate, share). Communion – placing everything together – can also mean uttering the truth throughout time and searching for the truth together: dialectics according to Plato. The dialectician is no specialist in hermeneutics, but he transports the essence of the world in his speech, looking for the noblest path of knowledge that man carries within. From *the Sophist,* we learn about the mission of the scholar to choose between those that are and those that are not, as long as the genders get mixed. Therefore, one cannot define man's journey by wasted possibilities: the historical being asserts itself wherever it finds itself. It is natural for us to assume an experience that connects us to the spirit and the significance of our historical life, not to the actual deed of our mundane life (a temporal accident). One form of dialectics – the first one, judging by importance and by meaning realizes the correspondence between those that exist and establishes their type in the live spirit of the dialogue. [30] Anyways, we cannot stop on the level of the dialogue from *the Sophist* because it is still far away from the true meaning of dialectics: its method unravels the principles, it makes us contemplate the essence (*Politeia*), and it brings sciences – according to their access to the being – to their natural hierarchy, claiming the top position. The final purpose of dialectics is to 'reach the

---

[29] Plato, *The Sophist*, translated by Nicholas P. White, in *idem, Complete Works,* edited, with Introduction and Notes, by John M. Cooper, associate editor D.S. Hutchinson (Indianapolis/Cambridge: Hacket Publishing Company, 1997), p. 282 (258 e).
[30] Ibid., 258 e–259 a.

oversensitive essence, The Good'. [31] Goodness allows contemplation; it can be entirely and equally distributed to each, but not shared. The target of dialectics has been long established, since Plato and his immediate commentators, but the way the dialogue is done could not evade a deep analysis. This analysis depicts dialectics as an essential quality for establishing truth within the domain of the being. The Greeks were especially fond of debate and oral research. Interrogation, the art of asking questions and mastering the meaning of words, is the most required quality for practising dialectics. *Sophistes,* just like most dialogues, keep us up to date on this and leads us to the essence of Plato's process for philosophical persuasion: a way to construe thinking and to approach the truth of the being in time, without any hidden intentions to distort the truth, like a sophist or like a false practitioner of the dialogue about principles.

However, we must keep in mind that the sophist's place in society from the historical time of the Academy is to distribute to his fellow members interested in listening and criticizing him a truth quite hard to grasp: reality is a mix of being and non-being, where difference and otherness must not be avoided but brought to light; they are the purpose of life, reason and metaphysics.

Asserting this actual situation without arguments and method (dialectics) is not just tactless but also lacks maturity when in contact with reality.[32] This is precisely why the sophist, who does not perform the method itself but a false art of the dialogue, wants to convince his opponent (partner) through persuasion. *To persuade* also leads to *coercion,* which could be an attitude proper for a philosopher, but also *an intention* to continue down a road using false arguments, like the case of a master of rhetoric, the discourse of a politician or the art of a poet. Meanwhile, dialectics is alive and spontaneous with no petty interests and persuades people through confidence and faith in the value of the principle because it is 'the one that reveals, through analysis, a base for knowledge; rhetoric is nothing but a subordinated science; [...] dialectics is truly a bright science.'[33]

Platonic dialectics is also eloquent proof for our topic because we propose to examine experience inside history and approach it like a spiritual communion. Dialectics covers most of the meaning we assign to historical communion in spirit and time. Compared to other ways of reaching communion with the being (the historical being in this case), the science of

---

[31] Constantin Noica, *Schiță pentru istoria lui Cum e cu putință ceva nou* (A Sketch for the history of How is something new possible), (Bucharest: Humanitas Publishing, 1995), p. 52.
[32] Plato, *Sophist,* 1997, 242 a–c.
[33] C. Noica, *Schiță pentru istoria lui Cum e cu putință ceva nou* , 1995, p. 50..

dialectic (disguised as the artistic type of dialogue, starting from principles and perfected in Plato's works) is more of a search and confession about the being. The way to do it is yet another argument that one must enter communion first through the word (logos) because it carries the truth and comes out of faith:

> Dialectics is more than just the science of prepared questions and answers. It is the science of pure spontaneity in the person asking the questions and the one answering them. Such a harsh punishment for writing to be under the word, which prohibits any spontaneity should make us question the importance Plato gives to all of the above. [34]

Dialectics and becoming

If we were to accept the primordial meaning of dialectics, the one before imposing the method as science (and art as well, the art of correct reasoning) by the Platonic doctrine, we would only be able to use its technical nature (gr. *dialegein*, from *legein,* to speak and *dia*, over, across). Dialectics was done exclusively through dialogue and uttering since it was the technique of arguing and dismissing through questions and answers. It was discovered by Zenon and practised by the followers of Socrates.

Dialectics tries to avoid any contradiction within the discourse and to make it difficult for the interlocutor while inviting him to search for the truth using masterly questions. It first needed to discover the false opinions and then incriminate them using a proliferating dialogue. Its first manifestation understood as such, took place before Socrates and consisted of the ability to discover falsities in a discourse. Since then, dialectics has increased its prestige, but not for its own sake, as *tekhne*, but rather through itself as an alive science, approaching and overcoming the purpose of maieutics[35]. Knowing yourself remains a Socratic wish – an urge from the spirit manifested in dialogue – the logos opens up to the person that listens and creates difficulties for himself (to the interlocutor as well) in receiving all at once because there is nothing to give through revelation. The Socratic meditation could be a way, but it does not come down to the monologue. In this instance, the dialogue is internal, hence the difficulty of bringing to light the latent virtues and simply remembering long-forgotten truths that lay deeply rooted – dormant – inside an untrained consciousness, unable to practice conversation with itself. Remembering is initiated through logos, or even better, through *dia-logos*, the agreement between thought and word.

---

[34] Ibid., pp. 50–51.
[35] C. Noica, *Schiță pentru istoria lui Cum e cu putință ceva nou*, 1995, pp. 47–48.

For Greek people, interior thinking (meditation) was an extension and an internalization of the dialogue.

Maieutics, or the doctrine of recollecting, creates difficulties when we try to value the traits of reasoning or the awakening of innate ideas into their universal path. 'Socrates' maieutics does not show us how to gain knowledge, nor how come the results we get are universal.'[36] This universality needs to be understood before it reflects the known reality as consensus and persuasion for those taking part in the dialogue, it must *become* logos that increases through uttering. 'The logos' belongs to consciousness because it represents communion; it is for everybody else and anytime. The dialogue – a word with myself and the citizens of the polis – becomes universal.

The original meaning of dialectics is communion in logos every time. It increases through uttering and has its own time (the logical time of logos), imagined by Noica as a circle of the becoming within being, unlike the linear one.

Dialectics is the path of uttering (and becoming) and logos within being; the fundamental question about being that Noica was inspired to formulate by a fragment from *Timaeus: ti to on men aei, genesin de ouk echon; kai ti to gignomenon men, on de oudepote* ('What is that which always is and has no becoming; and what is that which is always becoming and never is')[37]. After an analysis of the two sentences and the difficulties of translation, particularly in Latin and French, Alexandru Surdu underlines the importance of understanding these terms in context: *to on* and *genesin,* but also the lack of the verb *to be = eimi* in the first sentence, which is understandable in the original text because it would double *to on → eimi to on = to be being* and therefore have no sense. In French was inaccurately translated with *exists*[38]. Moreover, the term *genesis* also leaves space for interpretation. The Latin text uses *generatio* and the French *naître =* to beget, while in Romanian we have *devenire,* an existing term in French as well (*devenir*). *Genesis* references the first book of *Pentateuch* (birth, becoming), also mentioned by Noica in *Prima introducere* (*The First Introduction)* to *Devenirea întru ființă (Becoming within Being)*. For Plato, the being has no becoming. 'We must clearly establish the difference between Plato's concept and that of Noica,' says Alexandru Surdu.

---

[36] Ibid., p. 46.
[37] Plato, *Timaeos*, 1997, 27 d–28 a; See also Alexandru Surdu, *Comentarii la rostirea filosofică* (*Devenirea de dragul devenirii*), (Commentaries to philosophical uttering – Becoming for the sake of becoming), (Brașov: Kron-Art Publishing, 2009), p. 119.
[38] Ibid., p. 120.

Using "that which is always becoming", Plato refers to objects, things, corporal phenomena, the sensory perceptible, the whole Universe [...] created by the Demiurge (the creator) that can also destroy it at any moment. In other words, everything is always becoming but has no being.[39]

We do not wish to find arguments at any cost to prove that historical experience and dialectics (as they were understood and practised by the Greeks) had any contribution in strengthening the trust in the spiritual communion of the community, as well as in perpetuating the logos through ideative communication – forms of knowledge, moral norms etc. Everything mentioned has to do with the field of evidence. Logos is true, whole and present in the dialogue. The presence, that *is* made available by Plato for the dialogue and for the only way in which time participates in the being offers a purpose to our fleeting being. This purpose arises by taking part in the idea and inserting the truths across time inside the time that belongs to the word, a word carried by humans inside the community and searched in the logical time, as well as in the historical time. Presence is held back against becoming and the impoliteness of those who exist, able to destroy the order.

These all are parts of time, and *was* and *will be* are forms of time that have come to be. Such notions we unthinkingly but incorrectly apply to the everlasting being. For we say that it *was* and *is* and *will be,* but according to the true account only *is* is appropriately said of it. *Was* and *will be* are properly said about the becoming that passes in time, for these two are motions. But that which is always changeless and motionless cannot become either older or younger in the course of time – it neither ever became so, nor is it now such that it has become so, nor will it ever be so in the future. And all in all, none of the characteristics that becoming has bestowed upon the things that are borne about in the realm of perception are appropriate to it.[40]

Every move coordinated by the Demiurge for the general harmony of the Universe falls within becoming for becoming. However, the movement of dialectics evades time since *it was* and *will be* are deceiving forms of becoming, and becoming within being remains present (not necessarily in a time without becoming, like the eternity, but a time of the word that *is* anytime and anywhere).

This illusion of the disappearing time (neither the present actually *is* because, in real-time, it is a limit, infuriatingly thin, between the past and the future) goes from Plato through Aristotle and Saint Augustin to Kant.

---

[39] Ibid., p. 122.
[40] Plato, *Timaeos*, 1997, 37 e–38 b.

But why is time disconnecting and killing any impulse, choking life and disintegrating everything, even history? By walking reflection through some of the major landmarks mentioned above, time indeed dies because it is the time of revolution inside a baneful circle, the time of Kronos, according to Noica, not the time of Zeus and not yet the time of man.

For Plato, the time of dialectics is nothing like the time of history. History and ideas, Kronos and Zeus, the world grinding us, self-devouring and lost to oblivion (it does not exist in the communion with itself, nor with logos or the principles) retract the immortal forms. What is the reason for this rupture between reason and becoming, which neither Aristotle can restore? Why is history granted a purpose of disintegration and not one of establishment? According to Stagirite, this is because the universe is excluded from the individual, and if it exists (takes part) in the individual, the individual cannot withstand science.

However, Noica will prove that during the time of man (the uttering time), which also includes the time of history, logical time reunites the being enclosed by logos and makes it last in time as long as the time of history is not history as becoming, but a history continuously renewed for (within) the being. [41]

Noica questions the possibility for something to stay (in spirit, how the principles of ancient Greeks remain, for example) as reason stimulates its balance through a permanent new vision that determines the truth to belong to any time and, finally, to man. In doing so, he allows history to compensate for the apparent lack of becoming of the logos. Within becoming, everything is allowed, but nothing gets truly generated (it is not made), unless for those that are. And those that are, the humans, no longer become with every century of history that they always reclaim, but remain inside a history (it could also be the history of philosophy) which sometimes explains itself. Noica leaves it up to man to decide the distance he wants to impose regarding history, but this distance is never detached because history contains his being. It can neither be a positivist distance nor an existentialist one. The dialectics of history will never be a dialectics of existential actuality because it only allows one way of referencing history, proper to historicity, which

> sometimes renders it subjective to the point of transforming its century, while other times – even a certain objectivity is still a form of subjectivity – it pulls it further away just to be able to contemplate it better.[42]

---

[41] Constantin Noica, *Trei introduceri la devenirea întru ființă*, 1984.
[42] C. Noica, *Schiță pentru istoria lui Cum e cu putință ceva nou*, 1995, p. 9.

Initially, Noica incriminated history without any right to appeal, and he opposed culture to the geometrical spirit but he gradually became more nuanced and reinterpreted the becoming proper to history as a pillar, even for philosophy. He then discovered the circle of the true becoming, contained within a tetrad-type of dialectics focusing on the being.

> Noica attempts to draw synthesis of the triadic dialectics (of Hegelian type) with the Kantian tetrad-type dialectics (somewhat influenced by Thomas Aquinas as well). It makes it difficult to place his system in accurate fields of reality, especially the ontological ones. [43]

The Individual – "prisoner" of history

The perspective on being – eternal and immobile – is historically articulated and already in the mind of the individual still inside history. In a paper from 1943, Noica wrote about the three possible places of the individual in history. This paper was also a confession about the Romanian spirit[44] and gathers many notions (and forms) about Romanian descent in history. The need to construct (tend towards) historical types is gradual. Do we go towards history due to a destiny that determines the being of a community to settle in the place where it progresses, or do we create historical forms in order to go against becoming and hide from our destiny?

Historicity and truth seem to be two incompatible entities even though they assume each other, stand side by side and one after the other in the becoming, or at least they look for one another. The three possibilities mentioned by Noica (having as a pretext the works of other three great personalities: Neagoe Basarab, Dimitrie Cantemir and Lucian Blaga) become paradigmatic.

First, he mentions the subject (the obsession of modern-day Romanian culture, but especially of the one from between wars) of not wanting to remain the eternal villagers of history. Anything outside history refuses any possibility of the spirit finding itself. Leaving anonymity should be a

---

[43] Alexandru Surdu, *Cercetări logico-filosofice* (Logical and philosophical Researches), 2008, pp. 85–86.

[44] *Ce e etern şi ce e istoric în cultura românească* (What is eternal and what is historical in Romanian culture), conference held in 1943 in Berlin, titled *Die innere Spannung der Kleinen Kulturen*; in „Revista Fundaţiilor Regale" (The Magazine of the Royal Foundation), year X (1943), September, nr. 9, pp. 527–541; see Constantin Noica, *Istoricitate şi eternitate. Repere pentru o istorie a culturii româneşti* (Historicity and Eternity. Landmarks for a History of the Romanian Culture), edition supervised, Foreword and Bibliografy by Mircea Handoca (Bucharest: Capricorn Publishing, 1989).

personal, spontaneous and creative affirmation – getting closer to culture and further away from nature. The question Noica asks is the question of an entire generation – 'how can the "person" appear where … the category of personality is missing?'[45] Consequently, the individual looking for his roots assumes only halfway of the initial obsession because of the dilemma he has while choosing between the minor culture (where he gets consumed but also wants to affirm) and the major culture (where he fits in). The shapes of his history need to become outlining shapes first and then communicate and integrate those of universal history. The relation between individual and general, universal and particular, eternal and historical, becomes now a condition of history as a science; this is the condition of every culture and culture in general.

Permanences, everything outside history, the eternal, represent the gate before which the individual, decided to establish in time, remains quiet – he does not go in nor out, he grows old, but he does not feel the futility of each one of his deeds. Eternity is the time (it can also be 'times' that bends man but still cannot pull him out of silence or make him tell his history, much less do it) we all reference very humbly. Our will for history – and vocation – cannot detach from this modesty because this is how you distance yourself from the eternal and God. So, here we have a solution from the 16th century, proper to a decent and 'steady' mentality (efficient, we might say), which does not exclude action and is imposed by the spirit of the century and undertaken as such by Neagoe Basarab.

> The actual conflict between the eternal and the historical acquires a forward solution by giving up on the spirit or going around it, including everything it involves: knowledge, action, and human affirmation. Man does not assert himself here; he only has to confess. [46]

It is not a sin. It is a way of being and a way to relate to history. Times can come between people – it is a first step; separation means to recognise differences and conflict; separation first wakes up the will to argue, find solutions, and finally take action. The authority of argument – of spirit – or that of fact is not up for debate, is given. Can we state that, so far, our actions have been deliberately suspended? It would be a mistake, of course, because plans never overlap: 'wisdom', or better yet, detaching our thought from the world does not exclude man's settling into the world. Modesty and the fear of God do not exclude lucidity, bold actions or rationality. Religion aside, our voivodes built viable political and state entities, avails and laws inspired

---

[45] Ibid., p. 21.
[46] Ibid., p. 28.

by others or made *ad hoc* to help the state function and resist. The national being found its arguments and built its institutions. No institution lasts without a set of values or a culture to base on. The fact that many of them have disappeared and whatever is left to testify their existence does not form a national corpus for precise moments when history has been written, does not mean they did not exist. It does not mean we refused history or that she has renounced us, keeping us always on the side-line. Even if it was just a promise – there was a historical tension inside and outside – we have not kept away from it but used it to put things straight for ourselves. Perhaps the vibrations of the spirit were caused precisely by these tensions, even the concepts and our categories that enabled our becoming for us and others, the shapes of this becoming and our relationship with time. If you want to catch the move, you must sit where the scene allows you to observe without influencing the game. That is a condition for the critic and not necessarily for the spectator, who is already involved in the drama (the critic does not avoid it entirely either, but he can control the scenes, anticipate or suggest some moves). History was denied at first and then accepted. This acceptance is a move which no longer allows you to abandon everything through the back door if events take you by surprise. It is the place of the agent-historian (a concept used in Noica's text illustrated by Dimitrie Cantemir). He participates, judges, gets involved from the heart and criticises the Moldavian people in his writings, but not only. And just like him, there were other militant historians for about two centuries, until the independent state was founded and even beyond that, up to the Great Union.

There is a value scale that successively and contradictorily rises and descends, focused on its double-coiled axis (double spiral) between the transcendent and the immanent. There is an *axis dei* and an *axis mundis*. Everything that represents the values reflected by the transcendent gains meaning in opposition to the immanent. And the other way around – the symbols and deeds of this world cannot be understood without a variable beyond, while passing has no meaning except when related to eternal ideas. There are both ways, a *without which*, a complementarity whose support is the human: subject and predicate, shape and content, agent and instrument of the object trained on both sides of Reality.

To mediate the two worlds and achieve unity and purpose, one must give the creation an attribute of the creator. Here it is not about mediation nor an association and restrained alliance between the being and historical content, but a necessary construction inside the conscience – 'the tension created by the encounter between the eternal and the historical'[47]. Therefore, the two

---

[47] Ibid., p. 40.

meanings reunite. The concrete regains the value of experienced time. It is present, now for then – possible in the past, but in the future as well; it is also the person accounting for what it was because it is privileged to do so – an existing entity that knows itself without intermediates and also confesses about each time. [48]

Even though there are many more unities in the consciousness connecting the two dimensions, the historic reality gets captured when history enters consciousness. There is a logic of history which captures nature and man together as *a way of being* but not as an irreducible opposition, consensus or supplement of meaning. History and the world fuse; the principles of history become the principles of nature in general – the time of the integrating personality that unifies all cultures because they describe, as Blaga said, the 'interior stylistic enthusiasm' or the rhythms of the cultures and the becoming civilizations. An intuition captures this passage within. The essential is not doubting everything and then recover a bit of everything, a slice of existence with its shattered truth, but to harmonize worlds within your consciousness; the bits of existence opposed to the yearning of owning an intuition and a single truth – not the forms and not the laws; unity; 'the only thing deserving of our attention is not the truth, but subjecting truth to a process that will turn it into cosmos.' [49]

We exist inside history because we cannot quit encompassing the being with everything possible. The historical consciousness is self-consciousness, but historicity can alter introspection: in reality, the present becomes history. We have a moment to contemplate time only when we exit it. Still, we cannot conceive of becoming while we are inside it, only when we have already overcome it. This overcoming gets done in retrospect – our landmarks are here, but the landmarks of everyone before us have become an indifferent *here.* We are aware of the becoming between these moments but in retrospect. In the meantime, we also have the opportunity to create meaning. Our way (historic) is through evocation and self-suspension. But we can only detach by momentarily giving up on this moment (a complete life) or by transporting our time and filling it one time after another with the voices of the fulfilled time. But what would happen if we were to give up on the call that gets us closer to the present, and we would become the voice that brings together all the times, the tireless scream renewed throughout generations? The sign discovers the rhythm which turns its yet unseen face

---

[48] Vezi Mircea Florian, *Metafizica generală (Metafizică şi epistemologie)*, (General Metaphysics – Metaphysics and Epistemology), (Bucharest: Garamond Publishing, 1995), p. 164.
[49] Mircea Eliade, *Profetism românesc* (Romanian Prophecies), (Bucharest: Roza Vânturilor Publishing, 1990), p. 115.

to the present from the past; The continuous past. There is still a paradox: starting from the present each time, the man builds on his past with his eyes glued to the undefined horizon of the future. There is where he hastens his being and achieves his ideal. This 'wanderer of the being' gives up on his capital deposited inside an eternity he never parts with enough to rediscover his lost path towards being through history.[50] Thus, thrown in time and looking for meaning, he declares meanings and forgets the present from here for the one over there. That present is not actually entirely for his being; it is 'interrupted', fragmented and always indignant. He is always looking for a 'di-spelling', an incantation to escape time and to understand the appetite for time – for history. These *moire* (Moirai) that are intentionally (but most often not) pushing him towards his destiny, never at peace, to wander up and down – between the eternal and the flighty – are always determining him to give up on the now-perfect for the beyond-perfect, forever banished towards an elusive time. The Moirai, daughters of Zeus and Themis, decide man's destiny and make sure it gets fulfilled. Their decision is inexorable; even gods feared them. We must wonder: is not this blind push towards the time of the human being, forever damned to spend itself historically, carried out by the Moirai something we can also perceive from our inside, thanks to a way of being for the assumed historical time? Why not understand this wandering as a type of recovery? Why not see these Moirai as hidden resources from within, from the most profound part of us that determines the geometry of our souls, often distorted by the humane pathos? Why not see them as a will for shape, the Shape itself?

Greek mythology often perceived the Moirai negatively because they would hide the deeper purpose from us mortals, the ones transcending the humane and also the divine. This purpose would only get sorted in the end, as a tragical sentence. Maybe this is why the individual hides within history and revolts. He wavers between *logos* and *mythos* and turns to that wicked intelligence, the *mêtis.* This indirect alternative route is also through history, where the man thinks he can reclaim himself.

We must not set the geometrical spirit in opposition to the idea of historical becoming. These paths to knowledge must match, and maybe, by alternating between denial and participation in history, we could raise the barrier and discover the authentic time, the experience. In the end, the history of the time concept is the history of the question about the being of the being.[51]

---

[50] Emil Cioran, *Căderea în timp* (The Fall into Time), (Bucharest: Humanitas Publishing, 1999), pp. 16–19.

[51] Martin Heidegger, *History of the Concept of Time. Prolegomena*, translated by Theodore Kisiel (Bloomington: Indiana University Press, 1985), pp. 305–307.

We might find within the Moirai our predisposition to allow ourselves to get kidnapped by the experience that provides a historical trait rather than by the contemplation of ideas and essences. Could we find a refugee from the raw deed and the refusal of a rigid universe? It is also a lure for the calm spirits, those predisposed towards unity and able to notice the principle, to look for the perfect figure of an idea, the golden cut of thought or the geometrical course of reason inside history. But those spirits are also the lucid ones, and their affection for unity and non-contradiction leaves no room; everything gets consumed around the idea, and what is left, if anything, are those marks that get ignored by the geometer (the skilful architect), just like it would with simple residues from erecting a building. If there are no spoilages, they remain under the binder of the construction. That is why we must look at the building from the builder's perspective as well, or that of the accomplished novice, even the bricklayer. Just like historians, when they discover the foundations of a piece of a wall, and they restructure the draught of a monument using the humblest signs, hidden under the plaster, so do we need to re-grant the Idea and its architecture the instrument, even the dust left behind the construction of this theory.

Following a minimal acceptance of the past, each historic gesture means taking action in the value of the present. Precisely what Neagoe Basarab did when he recommended moderation in front of the world's struggle and its values that change according to the politics 'forged by the greatest'. He also recommended returning to the eternal and escaping the whirl of fleeting 'virtues'. Dimitrie Cantemir did the same. He descends with the confidence of a critic into the ferment of history and wishes to change its course. Blaga's attitude is not less involved but from a different level. He reunites the categories of the significance of culture with those of history, finding correspondences between stylistic fields and even transitions of shape between the non-history (pre-history) and history through substituted forms and ideas, revisited during historic time.[52] Mystery, for that matter, which also includes the historical being, cannot be deciphered, at least not during the historic time, unless assuming the risk of revealing that 'sacred path' man has to take to get saved along with his history.

The individual contemplates himself in the mirror and remains a prisoner of that image – he is more there, still there; he can only see himself sketching the geometry of a reflection. But is that him? A stranger to every sign, alienated by every gesture, he always remains in a calculated expectancy, waiting for an answer from who he thinks he sees. But is not

---

[52] Lucian Blaga, *Trilogia cosmologică* (The Cosmological Trilogy), (Bucharest: Minerva Publishing, 1974), p. 392.

his gesture, now, a little bit late? Isn't the tool he is using rendering precisely his intention? Isn't the present time, suspended, answering to the present of every image? Is history answering us according to our expectations? Between me and my one thousand recaptured reflections, am I still able to find myself? And where?

> As a presence, as a live fact, a given, the world is a presupposition of historical cultures, those in which the passing, destiny and actuality are most important. However, the world of geometrical-like cultures is an ideal of order done by human consciousness and kept by the human consciousness.[53]

But, on the contrary. We should not see passing here in the way we rebuild ourselves from an infinite number of possible ways, and none according to the perception of our aspirations historically developed. Duration has no meaning; neither does memory. Maybe the rhythm has meaning, the perspective gathered from other tens of meanings, the set connected to others, and vibration harmonizing with other vibrations, just like Pârvan, Xenopol and Conta all noticed. This is a fact recognized even by Noica, at the end of his writing, our pretext for everything written so far – the historical perspective put together by a Romanian (together with Blaga and the other three, but also Brătianu, Iorga and maybe Heliade-Rădulescu, Cantemir and many others like them) gets extended beyond history, to the entire universe. What else could Xenopol's history series be other than a way to connect human geometry while in historical becoming with the geometry of nature? What is history other than one of the two possibilities to see the world in its wholesomeness, 'the world of succession compared to the world of repetition'?[54]

The beginning belongs to each day, the present belongs to any time and non-history, the eternal able to freeze any movement, returns with every word of the individual in history, with every utopia – 'one thousand years we have stepped on spikes, and we will still step on them for a long time'[55] – only to realize it has not yet pulled apart from time. Destiny is there, present in one thousand lives and moments, but the individual is present in history like through a net.

---

[53] C. Noica, *Mathesis sau bucuriile simple* (Mathesis or the Simple Joys), (Bucharest: Fundaţia pentru Literatură şi Artă „Regele Carol al II-lea" Publishing, 1934), p. 16.
[54] A.D. Xenopol, *Principiile fundamentale ale istoriei* (The Fundamental Principles of History), (Bucharest: Albatros Publishing, 2003), p. 61.
[55] Emil Cioran, *Schimbarea la faţă a României* (The Transfiguration of Romania), (Bucharest: Humanitas Publishing, 1990), p. 99.

History and truth

There is a saying, apparently paradoxical, formulated to underline the difference between *the historical capacity to pursue the proceedings* (the relativity of truths established in time) and the absolute truth of principles, established beyond contrasts and the original or factual references to the event (or experience) and goes like this 'History is fatal to philosophy.' [56] According to a semi-general opinion, within the philosophy that references becoming and its principles, history (not in its theoretical form) is shaped and subdued by time; its truths get expressed by personalities and cultures – and thus, the reference to historical 'cultures' of facts. 'The relativist cohesion of philosophy to the historical becoming transformed *historicism* into a guillotine of any systematic thought.' [57]

Confronting truth with becoming is not a methodological error in itself, but for sciences, like history, this is an adapting principle to a context outside of which truth – the historical fact and its general social significance – does not work. But opposing the history of philosophy is a stand that does not even belong to a historian, much less to a researcher. The singular – the individual's significance inside history is closer to the value of the fact itself for the epistemology of social sciences, including the philosophy of history – is not contradicting the general from the science of history. However, the opposition between history and philosophy signifies more than methodology, even epistemology. It comes back to a generally accepted attitude starting with the Enlightenment but became common knowledge in the second part of the 19th century, when social sciences, especially history, were looking for their foundation. The first echoes on this matter came from positivism, and they meant to overcome metaphysical speculations.

Unfortunately, the history of philosophy does not seem to have enough confidence to create connections between doctrines, thoughts and systems therefore, the tendency to give a relative trait and to methodologically 'twist' the criteria of truth, turning the principles anchored in metaphysics into something profane. Another tendency is to forget that

> generalizing history is not a theatrical blow for modern consciousness, but the inevitable result of convergent and tireless efforts to decipher the meaning of the doctrines of philosophy.' [58]

---

[56] Mircea Florian, *Experienţa ca principiu de reconstrucţie filosofică* (Experience as Principle of Philosophical Reconstruction), (Bucharest: Gramar Publishing, 2002), pp. 187–204.

[57] Ibid., p. 187.

[58] Ibid., p. 188.

Of course, Hegel offers a much more appropriate solution for the spirit of Time: the dialectics of ideas and reason to which he attaches the historical capacity to pursue the proceedings – the dynamism – which momentarily redeems the autonomy of philosophy from a metaphysical perspective. But the idea must bring historicism its legitimacy concerning the crooked theoretical mission by configuring history within the classical scientific approach (inserting into the universal) and establishing meaningful sentences for times when the historical process will not get the support of a historical document. That is where the logic of history intervenes – one of contradiction – and the autonomy of history surpasses that of 'cultures' formed based on the theory of history. Those who have tried to relate history to a system – of science or autonomous, similar to philosophy – have never concluded. They did, however, create the premises for reconciliation between historicity and truth.

Besides Hegel – from a certain perspective, he is the only one able to maintain the balance between becoming and reason by postulating identity: *History is the revelation of the Absolute*[59] – others have attained the epistemic reconciliation and the ontic conversion of the historic fact beyond the false antinomy between absolutism and relativism: Wilhelm Dilthey, Wilhelm Windelband and Heinrich Rickert. Historicism must escape the dilemma formed within the evolution of modern trends: the strict independence of philosophy from history or even worse, the complete dependence of philosophy on history.[60] By silencing the conflicts (and not camouflaging them under weak speculations that bring out the historic trait), we must notice that it is difficult to translate the opposition between philosophy (eternal truth) and history ('living' the truth) only using epistemological terms. The 'phobia' towards history also has an anthropological explication. By accepting a certain periodicity (annual cycles or extended to include periods established according to archetypal events), we were able to build traditional cultures that contradict the historical evolution. 'The eternal repetition' supports human destiny because, without discovering the temptation of getting involved in history, it has a cultural sense of conserving important events and giving them an archetypal value. Time recovers destiny, not history: the cycle symbolically ends precisely where it began. The real event gains mythical importance while time has another rhythm, of course – everything references 'that time', ab origine, including the historical agent which retracts itself from the world's historical capacity to pursue the proceedings. This gesture

---

[59] Ibid.
[60] Ibid., p. 191.

creates a bridge, a significant identity between two realities, where the first one has a constitutive meaning (in illo tempore). Mircea Eliade closely analysed how the antique spirituality relates to the historic event, unravelling the passing of essence (value) from the historical present into the archetypal one, where the archaic man knows no deeds that have not been accomplished or previously lived by another, *one that was not human*. Everything is done according to the characteristics of primitive cultures and referencing the Sacred because everything is replayed due to everything that was once done, once becoming here an authentic, real-time.[61]

We must ask ourselves: if history gets abolished, are the premises of absolving the deed from the real threat represented by the present set? This deed, historical in essence – engaged in an interpretation by means from within science – gets impregnated with the prosaism and inefficiency of day-to-day acts. What value can the non-liberty of the 'done' deed have concerning the liberty made easy to identify by time – discursive freedom, fundamental – even if the deed references the archetypal act? Of course, from the perspective of a compromise and from within a sui-generis historicism, any gesture can evoke a cultural act. The event confirms the Idea and each historical event – the will of the universal Spirit, the reason why Hegel, for example, can understand 'reading the morning newspaper as a sort of a realist blessing' of the Idea getting confirmed every day.[62]

However, history follows its own rules. We have mentioned earlier that this type of solution, where the historical point of view – the theory's print on fact – is not limited to being just an interpretation comes from W. Dilthey. According to Mircea Florian, Dilthey understood the side of history able to criticize it as an 'introduction' of a discourse on the historical fact within the limits of a philosophical perception. Aware or not, he did not understand it as a scientific abstraction, hollow and indifferent, nor as an effective layout based on rigid principles. Then again, we cannot overcome the already mentioned dilemma because this organizing still has a flaw:

> either knowing the various cultural structures is also a structure connected to time – and in this case, it drowns in historicism – or it is no longer dependent on a historical structure, and thus, philosophy begins only after overcoming the historic conditions and the vital reactions.[63]

---

[61] Mircea Eliade, *The Myth of the Eternal Return*, translated from French by Willard R. Trask (New York: Harper & Brothers Publishers, 1959), pp. VII-VIII.

[62] Ibid., p. 142.

[63] M. Florian, *The Myth of the Eternal Return*, 1959, p. 192.

Mircea Florian finds yet another methodological justification towards a resemblance between the ability to render a system and the historical capacity to pursue the proceedings: there is a return on both sides to a fundamental theoretical correspondence, a bridge between Hegel's philosophy and the German neo-Kantism, which (especially the first one) confirms the thesis of an inseparable connection between history and philosophy. This connection is not to be understood as a one-sided dependence (philosophy becomes unambiguous in history) but as an ambivalence – historicity (a trait of the doctrines) cannot negate the independence and the supra-historic characteristic of philosophy.[64] The cohesion comes from the fact that both reach a *problem*, a dynamic element that acts as a catalyst of the system because 'the problem is never scholastic, but the solution is always systematic.'[65]

That is true for Noica as well. Historicity creates the premises (the becoming) for philosophy in the modern era, post-Hegelian. That always gets done from the irrational it has regularly referenced, as an extension of the *real* dialogue (the result of determined chaos) that can also be prompted by history. This irrationality is the *given* – just like other times it was the irrational of theology or that of science – or the becoming trying to get back to itself, the being. Besides and beyond Plato's philosophy, or the Greeks who did not require perversion nor chaos, there is a contradiction meant to allow philosophy to be reborn and get back to itself out of being time.

> If the logos of theology contradict themselves, then it goes back to the Middle Ages to the theological irrational (respectively from the "logicity" of theology); if there is also any logos of science at play, contradicting each other, then it starts from the chaos of science; if they belong to becoming (cosmic, organic, spiritual), it will start from history or its becoming, just like today.[66]

Therefore, there are two starting points – the irrational and the chaos, which both make history possible in a philosophical way and *the problem*, the essence, the pattern of support and stimulation of the system. There are places where history provokes philosophy, offers concepts and finds solutions. And not just momentary solutions but bridges, landmarks of the discourse based on which real connections can establish between the universal and the particular rising from history. There is also a permanent

---

[64] Ibid.
[65] Ibid.
[66] Constantin Noica, *Trei introduceri la devenirea întru ființă* (Three Introductions to the Becoming Within Being), 1984, p. 56.

referencing of time and the dimension of temporality through the becoming and its contradictions, as well as the problems that give meaning (and substance) to the system, and open a supra-historic perspective for history through philosophy – a perspective from beyond, but still from within time, not from the values of the non-history. Hence, without obstructing philosophy, history offers a place – occasion – to get set/recover in time.

> The awareness of the historic becoming is, after all, what we have more than Plato and even Hegel, for whom the Spirit became absolute again. Just by means of this awareness, we dare make philosophy after and beyond them.[67]

We can say that these are two of the proper times when philosophy truly meets time. History tries as well, by defying its eternal truths or challenging them to solve fundamental contradictions that seem to undermine its being – the historical being itself is an uttered *no* in front of the non-becoming but existing being. The historic being is provocative through the irrational path towards history and the historicity opposite to reason and self-knowledge, attainable only through philosophy; 'when someone is doing philosophy, they need to step into chaos and feel comfortable there.'[68] But nobody descends deliberately when they know they cannot measure alone with an icon, even an archetype, idea or some form of self-becoming that they can detach from themselves and offer it to the eternal thought, the logos. That is the only way we can be sure that historicity and becoming, in time and beyond time, remain challenges, authentic reasons to do philosophy. As Noica put it best:

> History changes not only our perspective while doing philosophy but also the *object* of philosophy. We no longer philosophize about the world seen from a theological perspective nor about one seen purely from a scientific angle, but we must do it about the "historic becoming".[69]

References

Aristotle. 1963. *Categories and De Interpretatione*, translated with Notes by J.L. Ackrill, Clarendon Aristotle Series, general editors J.L. Ackrill and Lindsay Judson. New York: Oxford University Press.

---

[67] Ibid., p. 59.
[68] Ludwig Wittgenstein, *Însemnări postume (Post-mortem Notes)*, 1914–1951, translated from English by Mircea Flonta and Adrian-Paul Iliescu (Bucharest: Humanitas Publishing, 2005), p. 128.
[69] C. Noica., *op. cit.*, p. 59.

Aristotle. 2016. *Metaphysics*, translated with Introduction and Notes by C.D.C. Reeve. Indianopolis/Cambridge: Hackett Publishing Company, Inc.

Bălan, Sergiu. 2009. *Între istorie și filosofie. Sistemul lui R. G. Collingwood* (Between history and philosophy. The system of R. G. Collingwood). Bucharest: Publishing of the Romanian Academy.

Blaga, Lucian. 1974. *Trilogia cosmologică* (The Cosmological Trilogy). Bucharest: Minerva Publishing.

Cioran, Emil. 1990. *Schimbarea la față a României* (The Transfiguration of Romania). Bucharest: Humanitas Publishing.

Cioran, Emil. 1999. *Căderea în timp* (The Fall into Time). Bucharest: Humanitas Publishing.

Djuvara, Neagu. 2008. *Există istorie adevărată? Despre „relativitatea generală" a istoriei. Eseu de epistemologie* (Is there a true history? On "the general relativity" of history. Epistemology essay). Bucharest: Humanitas Publishing.

Eliade, Mircea. 1959. *The Myth of The Eternal Return,* translated from the French by Willard R. Trask. New York: Harper & Brothers Publishers.

Eliade, Mircea. 1990. *Profetism românesc* (Romanian Prophecies). Bucharest: Roza Vânturilor Publishing.

Florian, Mircea. 1995. *Metafizica generală* (Metafizică și epistemologie), (General Metaphysics – Metaphysics and Epistemology). Bucharest: Garamond Publishing.

Florian, Mircea. 2002. *Paradoxele experienței* (The Paradoxes of Experience), in *Experiența ca principiu de reconstrucție filosofică* (Experience as a principle of philosophical reconstruction. Bucharest: Gramar Publishing.

Florian, Mircea. 2003. *Recesivitatea ca structură a lumii* (Retraction as structure of the world), vol. I. Bucharest: Publishing of Pro Foundation.

Heidegger, Martin. 1985. *History of the Concept of Time. Prolegomena*, translated by Theodore Kisiel. Bloomington: Indiana University Press.

Kant, Immanuel. 1998. *Critique of pure reason,* translated and edited by Paul Guyer, University of Pensylvania, Allen W. Wood, Yale University. Cambridge University Press.

Noica, Constantin. 1934. *Mathesis sau bucuriile simple* (Mathesis or the Simple Joys). Bucharest: Fundația pentru Literatură și Artă „Regele Carol al II-lea" Publishing.

Noica, Constantin. 1943. *Ce e etern și ce e istoric în cultura românească* (What is eternal and what is historical in Romanian culture), conference held in 1943 in Berlin, titled *Die innere Spannung der Kleinen Kulturen*;

in „Revista Fundaţiilor Regale" (The Magazine of the Royal Foundation), year X (1943), September, nr. 9, p. 527–541.

Noica, Constantin. 1984. *Trei introduceri la devenire întru fiinţă* (Three Introductions for Becoming Within Being). Bucharest: University Publishing.

Noica, Constantin. 1989. *Istoricitate şi eternitate. Repere pentru o istorie a culturii româneşti* (Historicity and Eternity. Landmarks for a History of the Romanian Culture), edition supervised, Foreword and Bibliography by Mircea Handoca. Bucharest: Capricorn Publishing.

Noica, Constantin. 1995. *Schiţă pentru istoria lui Cum e cu putinţă ceva nou* (A Sketch for the history of How is something new possible). Bucharest: Humanitas Publishing.

Popa, Mihai. 2008. *Individul – „prizonier al istoriei"* (The Individual – „a captive of history"), in *Studii de istorie a filosofiei româneşti* (Studies on the History of Romanian Philosophy), vol. III, *Omagiu profesorului Alexandru Surdu* (An Homage to professor Alexandru Surdu), coordinated by Viorel Cernica, ed. Supervised by Mona Mamulea. Bucharest: Publishing House of the Romanian Academy.

Plato. 1997. *Timaeos*, in *idem, Complete Works,* edited, with Introduction and Notes, by John M. Cooper, associate editor D.S. Hutchinson. Indianapolis/Cambridge: Hacket Publishing Company.

Plato. *Sophist*. 1997. Translated by Nicholas P. White, in *idem, Complete Works,* edited, with Introduction and Notes, by John M. Cooper, associate editor D.S. Hutchinson. Indianapolis/Cambridge: Hacket Publishing Company.

Plato, *Timaeos*. 1997. Translated by Donald J. Zeyl, in *idem, Complete Works,* edited, with Introduction and Notes, by John M. Cooper, associate editor D.S. Hutchinson. Indianapolis/Cambridge: Hacket Publishing Company.

Surdu, Alexandru. 2008. *Cercetări logico-filosofice* (Logico-philosophical Researches), edition supervised by Victor Emanuel Gica, Dragoş Popescu, Ovidiu Grama. Bucharest: Technical Publishing.

Surdu Alexandru. 2009. *Comentarii la rostirea filosofică* (*Devenirea de dragul devenirii*), (Commentaries to philosophical uttering – Becoming for the sake of becoming). Braşov: Kron-Art Publishing.

Wittgenstein, Ludwig. 2005. *Însemnări postume* (Post-mortem Notes), 1914–1951, translated from English by Mircea Flonta and Adrian-Paul Iliescu. Bucharest: Humanitas Publishing.

Xenopol, Alexandru Dimitrie. 2003. *Principiile fundamentale ale istoriei* (The Fundamental Principles of History). Bucharest: Albatross Publishing.

CHAPTER III

CONSTANTIN NOICA ON EVOLUTION AND CIRCULARITY

Chronology and becoming within history

To establish the specificity of the relation between the two concepts, we will choose the same straight path Noica chose to introduce us to the circularity of being. The *Three Introductions to Becoming Within Being (Trei introduceri la devenirea întru ființă)* will help us simplify the journey we announced in the title, as there is also a middle way to reach our target: *The Time of Stimulated Becoming (Timpul devenirii stimulate)* and its second introduction, which momentarily disrupts the circularity outlined in *Becoming Within Being (Devenirea întru ființă)*, enough to show us the meaning of true becoming. The structure of *Becoming Within Being* is absorbed here by the becoming of thought and the philosophical conscience, which gets to enter its own time utilising the becoming itself, the history. *The Uttering Time (Timpul rostitor)* offers Noica a reason for true evolution – beyond the rhythms of nature –, the evolution of spirit, searching for itself out of fear of becoming redundant: the motif of 'How is something new possible' 'sets us in the stream of life of the spirit, one of the principles that can unify the history of philosophy. [1] Inside this 'How is something new possible' we can actually find the possibility of evolution overpassing the pure and simple evolution from nature, particularly of the organic world, but still relying on it. Real-time, which means demolition and entropy, originating from the present and collapsing (dying) into the past, gives evolution its relativism in nature. The persistence of change (despite the rhythm that resets periodically) gives the specie (the genome) the chance to survive; in time, the genes pick up on the frequency of this relative change,

---

[1] Constantin Noica, *Schiță pentru istoria lui Cum e cu putință ceva nou* (A Sketch for the history of How is something new possible), (Bucharest: Humanitas Publishing, 1995), p. 15.

namely the beneficial changes of the specie.[2] For Noica, time is inseparable from becoming: a time of becoming within becoming, *the real* or *circular time,* and the time of becoming within being, the time of man or the time of thought (of the being), that which sets things in place, the *uttering time.*[3]

Natural time and logical time

Real-time is the time of nature. It is also the time of man, unable to surpass the possibilities of biology. According to Aristotle, there is a causative and mathematical recurrence (rotation) setting up the forms of time or the number of movements after anterior and posterior. Revolving time means chronology and natural law. It can get reduced to a formula and a rhythm because it fits the number. This time of Kronos (chronology) originates and dissipates into the present in the name of both past and future, without leaving the becoming within becoming: cosmic time, solar time, the time of the year (weather), organic time, the time of history, psychic time. As for the time of history, we must note that the availability towards being can come from history through cultural evolution. In his first *Introduction,* Noica confronts history with the evolution of thought; becoming within history is the fountain of philosophy. History stirs logical chaos, which generates philosophy.

> If theology's logos are the ones contradicting themselves, then it [philosophical consciousness – A/N, M.P.] begins in the Medieval Era from the theological irrational (namely from the «logic» of theology); if at stake are the logos of science, contradicting themselves, then it starts from the chaos of science; if they belong to becoming (cosmic, organic, spiritual), it will start from history, or its becoming, as it is. [4]

Logical time (a type of uttering time) distorts the idea of time. It deforms time. First, it is the time of questions we must ask and answer. Sometimes, the answer precedes the question. No matter how compressed, it can still create the illusion of simultaneity, and it exists. The program of a calculus machine is a compressed time, which includes the necessary time to formulate logical systems.

---

[2] Robert N. Brandon, *Evolution*, în "Philosophie of Science", vol. 45, no. 1 (Mar., 1978), pp. 96–109.
[3] C. Noica, *Trei introduceri la devenirea întru fiinţă* (Three Introductions to Becoming Within Being), (Bucharest: Univers Publishing, 1984), p. 92.
[4] C. Noica, *Trei introduceri la devenirea întru fiinţă*, 1984, p. 36.

This time cannot be neutralized: electronic devices have shortened calculus amazingly, but they have only shortened it. You need time for any process or operation, an operational time, just like you need some time for any establishment. [5]

If we analyse just the form of logical time, we notice it is consubstantial to human history, the becoming within being. But 'the revolution' of history became visible in 1800 when the premises for an authentic history got established, as Noica puts it. Before that, the entire history was a sort of *to be in*: 'to be in nature, in geography, in religions, in destiny.' [6] To be in nature, not against nature, as Noica explains. In the extension of nature, philosophy is also possible. That is precisely how Romanian philosophy is. We will see this later when we include Conta, Xenopol and Blaga. [7] Ancient Greek philosophy and German Idealism are against nature. The spirit rebels against nature, thus creating the time and space where it can exist. Logical time, that of logos has different traits from real-time: 1. It only has two dimensions, past and future, lacking present; 2. It can be compressed or extended without limits; 3. It has direction, but it is not irreversible; 4. Unlike real-time, it can always be resumed.[8] The nature of uttering time, in its highest degree, the time of becoming within being, operates man's conscious and his real creations (spiritual works, actual works – materials – which incorporate a spirit, like a machine) inside the history as becoming *within* the culture. Its nature is derived from the nature of real-time, but it changes the course and the essence of the basic principles of the latter. It is not a cardinal number or a measure of movement, but order and not so much an order of succession, as it is a sequence. Lastly, it is a connection in succession. This last trait is surprising because it gets us close to the definition of Xenopol's causative sequence, which 'distorts' nature in history: the historical set.

Connection and circularity. Evolution

Connectivity represents the purpose and the openness of human nature. Circularity is a bond with a focus on the future. Paradoxically, the history of *being within* is grounded in the future, not the past, or the present, which suspends bonds. The time of Kronos (who kills his offspring) is certainly real

---

[5] Ibid., p. 94.
[6] Ibid., p. 134.
[7] Idem, *Pagini despre sufletul românesc* (Pages on the Romanian Spirit), (Bucharest: Humanitas Publishing, 1995), pp. 73–100.
[8] Idem, *Trei introduceri la devenirea întru ființă*, 1984, p. 103.

time, says Noica. It is the time of nature, scourging man's expectations and offering him infinite and incomprehensible past and future. Evolution is not an issue for this infinity. It sits frozen, focused on the present, while the purpose of logos (giving meaning to the becoming) is to decrease and negate the universal entropy. The imbalance of being within negates the present time of movement by replacing the uniformly accelerated rectilinear motion law with the law of absorbing the becoming within being, the real (humane) sign of history.

Circularity defies the present. No purpose of circularity could have been achieved by the later modern era because this era thought about a dump becoming as becoming within becoming, an interpretation wronged twice.

> It is certain that, instead of a warning, Noica offers a prediction. The foundation of this in modern philosophy could be a double misrepresentation: one of the becoming, and the second of the being. Noica assures us that becoming was conceived as birth and death and as their mechanical repetition; the being got conceived as torn from any type of becoming. [9]

Still, Noica will find forerunners for the notion of becoming within being. One of them is Plato. In his works, he defines becoming in his terms, largely as a circularity, where everything gets fixed at the level of ideas, an existence 'without birth or death'. But it seems that this becoming cannot solve the category 'scheme' like the author of *Becoming within being* wanted, because the Greeks, Plato included, had no concept of time to link it to the being, nor had they the notion of becoming within. The first clear concept of becoming in connection with time came from Aristotle. The traits he used to define time and elaborate the system of categories have remained valid up until the early Modern Era. However, he still had not reached the inner being. Even though for Aristotle the being came first and sciences were arranged according to the way they access the being, with philosophy being entitled (since 'it does not see the being as something other than the being'), knowledge is yet moulded after ontology. Reversing the rapport is strictly Kantian. 'That Aristotle starts from defining the being to later on reaching the possibility of knowledge, while Kant, on the contrary, starts from defining the factors of knowledge, is a statement whose truth we cannot deny.' [10]

---

[9] Alexandru Surdu, *Vocaţii filosofice româneşti* (Romanian philosophical vocations), (Bucharest: Romanian Academy Publishing, 1995), p. 96.
[10] C. Noica, *Schiţă pentru istoria lui Cum e cu putinţă ceva nou,* 1995, p. 97.

We think that one of the solutions for Noica's evolution is how uttering time preserves the results of becoming while acknowledging the spiritually stimulated becoming. The attributes of logical time reinforce this opinion; firstly, there is a lack of present time, therefore, an imbalance. If we analyse, in general, the results of the evolution, we notice a statistical balance among temporal coordinates. The 'gravitational' centre of them is the present, taken as a landmark to serve real-time. The present signalises the cases and the options (regarding the past and the future) that are valid to do an overview configuration of a process or a system. No matter its form, we can say that present is the ultimate form of evolution. One of the leading factors to a decrease in trusting the heuristic and the theoretical possibilities of the concept was the anthropocentrism in the structure of evolutionism (otherwise, a defect any concept needs to bear when it gets extended outside the theoretical possibilities for which its emergence was necessary). It was believed that the human mind has a predisposition to thinking in an evolutionist way. Thus, it can conjugate the time of all its existences (biological, technical, historical) with human expectancies and possibilities of its history. This status usually finds itself in a clear separation from reality. [11] Otherwise, we cannot negate the contribution of evolutionism in detaching social studies from the mechanistic and universal paradigm of general studies in the second half of the 19th century. History's method claims evolution (and progress) as one of the fundamental concepts we can use to think about history. We cannot make or think about history without the direction of all the changes because this offers unity in a sea of rather chaotic changes.[12] However, seeing the evolution from a phylogenetic perspective reveals its anchor in ontogenesis and its focus on the present time of the individual. Despite the relativity of the perspective of history and its related sciences, evolution involves a particular temporality, thought about only in becoming. Noica's concept of becoming and the circularity where this concept is claimed brings evolution into different patterns, logical this time.

> It has appeared, together with logical time, a new form of temporality that does not focus on the present. It lacks determined measure, but at the same time, proves to be sure of itself while also proving to be capable of a restart at any time. [13]

---

[11] Pierre L. van den Berghe, *Why Mast Sociologists Don't (and Won't) Think Evolutionary*, in "Sociological Forum", vol. 5, no. 2 (Iun., 1990), p. 175.
[12] Raymond Aron, *Introducere în filosofia istoriei* (Introduction to the philosophy of history), (Bucharest: Humanitas Publishing, 1997), p. 181.
[13] C. Noica, *Trei introduceri la devenirea întru ființă*, 1984, p. 112.

Indeed, the potential of circularity as becoming within being resumes itself into the traits of logical time, which outlines man's possibilities to approach history and release it from the influence of a periodicity without meaning (from under the meaning of to be in).

The Antinomies of Spiritual Becoming

Real-time and logical time intersect within the human being. The natural being residing inside the human must connect with the spiritual controlled by language. Noica puts inside this coincidence, which sometimes resolves itself through conflict, all the other contradictions specific to human nature and the historical way of being. One of the first antinomies is that between soul and spirit. The soul relates to reality. It is answer and adaptation continuously controlled by natural conditions. The spirit still refuses to subordinate to Kronos' time. 'The soul divides, the spirit unites'.[14] The orientation of each (soul and spirit) is being disputed inside the man in an antinomic way, or as Mircea Florian said, receding (in this case, recession belongs to the spirit).

We can also label the antinomies described by Noica as an intimate input of becoming. Their purpose is to record the inevitable tensions that occur when the two forms of time overlap. They all manifest on the social level. Besides the already mentioned binomial soul-spirit, we also have the antinomies feminine/masculine, body/spirit, and nature/ culture, that coexist in a sort of existential 'conflict', seemingly unsolvable and unable to resolve itself within the culture. Everything Noica wrote opens with a prologue meant to underline the historical significance of the thesis that needs to be extended throughout all the continents of the spirit (if we can see within the cultural development of an idea, an individualised topos of meanings having conceptual borders moderately outlined: The Greek spirit and that of medieval Christian Europe, different in its ideatic 'geography' from the modern or contemporary spiritual reality). As a matter of fact, in all of his important works, as well as in his complete studies, Noica maintains the connections – always renewed within the idea – with all these 'monarchs' of culture, which he directly interrogates, often breaking down their systems in his approach, trying to get the essence, the truth and the strong ideas from other people's thoughts. It is also the case of *Timpul devenirii stimulate (The Time of Stimulated Becoming)* when Goethe (actually Faust, his masterpiece) gets interrogated about the becoming within being. Faust II allows Noica to 'stage' the drama of the encounter between nature and

---

[14] Ibid., p. 114.

culture, between 'the small world' (Goethe's words) and the big world of the spirit, saved mostly for the second part of the already mentioned work. This conflict – which according to Noica, it has been profoundly experienced by Goethe when he admitted in front of Eckermann 'that he cannot see any connection […] between the five acts of the second part' – exists because Noica believes that Faust lives inside the logical time. Having already been through the small history of the first part and an important part of his own life, the pact Faust agrees to is the rejection of the present, the denial of the moment in the name of the great culture.

> He never knew any form of present, so he dares the devil to give him one, thus pulling him out of his logical time and throwing him into real-time, making him say this to a moment: «Stay». He used to live in a time of awareness, where that which still does not exist could be more real than what exists in the present moment. [15]

Therefore, Faust is an example of evolution (the becoming of self through philosophy and culture). Driven by the intimate ways of free and natural becoming, the human individual cannot make history without certain waivers. For Faust, this signifies giving up the seduction of nature in favour of the tempting culture. As a matter of fact, there are five Faustian lures, but the cultural one prevails and saves him in the end, even though the ultimate lure in this character's outline of self-becoming (and giving up on the pact) is the political one from the 5th act. The other three lures (economic power, scientific power and military power) are nothing but reinforcements for the energies of the spirit to face destiny. This time destiny is not dictated by gods, nor by a Moira from beyond nature and law, but by a destiny incorporated in the substance of his own individuality, where the becoming is established by promoting the intimate vocational pattern, able to draw human nature closer to the cultural essence of the human becoming.[16] This becoming is consciously set towards the future; the history of the individual is denied to the low becoming by the circular time and pushed towards the human being glanced at through history as an opening. 'The human being without a present, uttering, not just circular, out of plenitude and not of deficit, the man, on the other hand, is an active bearer of the future.'[17] Therefore, anything that is potentially natural within man sustains the

---

[15] Ibid., p. 122.

[16] Constantin Rădulescu-Motru, *Opere alese* (Selected Works), vol. II, *Vocaţia. Factor hotărâtor în cultura popoarelor. Timp şi destin* (Vocation. Crucial factor in the culture of peoples. Time and destiny), (Bucharest: Publishing House of the Romanian Academy, 2006), pp. 186–2002.

[17] C. Noica, *Trei introduceri la devenirea întru fiinţă*, 1984, p. 125.

evolution towards the being of culture that exists within, the geometrical expansion of thought (which can sometimes become a dangerous game), a pact with the devil in a Faustian sense, but with a spiritual essence, not out of a natural temptation. Goethe uses Faust to fight off 'piety without religion' because this is the book of lucidity without useless devotions, the 'book of culture, up to artificial and man-made nature.' It is yet another proof that Noica's man *utters himself* through history, that history is openness towards the being.

Circularity – a way to recover history?

The historical being attempts to avoid the contingent through the duration of cultural values, the configuration of historical cycles and by applying to the transcendent. The philosophy of history deals mostly with these aspects, while the theory of history, as an epistemology and reference to the forms of both historical knowledge and the fundamental principles of history as science, discusses more the logical and methodological norms and less on the principles of becoming itself. The theory of history is adjacent to the paradigm of the universal sciences, even though it is frequently pondered upon if it can be considered one of these sciences and whether it interrogates the general or limits itself to describing unique, non-recurring deeds. Without a doubt, the general exists within history (for example, the historical laws), but there is also history within all the sciences; knowledge itself is *becoming*, it adapts to reality and becomes its possession, together with all of its forms – elevated to the level of principles. The contrast between the philosophy of history and its theory becomes prominent when we acknowledge that the first one deals with principles, while the second one is a critique of the methods of knowledge. The philosophy of history goes back to the original form of the questions and it forgets about the auxiliary, the collateral and the fleeting, remembering just the essential, the laws of becoming – an attitude recommended by both Leibniz and Noica.[18]

Thanks to this attitude of recovering the general, Noica's demand – 'Rid yourselves of history!' – paradoxically becomes the sign and value of historical reason, giving back to the being its time-transfigured face and the becoming it searches for. In order to reach the being we must set aside and forget all the residual elements. Forgetting these elements is the way to enter the circle of becoming, avoiding its foolish flow, where waters are still not

---

[18] Constantin Noica, *Mathesis sau bucuriile simple* (Mathesis or the simple joys), (Bucharest: The Foundation for Literature and Art "Regele Carol al II-lea", 1934), p. 39.

set apart: 'The living waters and the dead waters of history – who can tell them apart today when everything still flows?' [19]

Circularity is one aspect of becoming, ever since Vico mentioned *corsi e ricorsi.* The subject of circularity[20] requires an 'arrival' to the initiation point of becoming, but not just a simple 'arrival'; it's more of a *confirmation* of a path whose *affirmation* exists right from the start. In other words, the beginning and the end coincide. We say 'arrival', not arrival to something because the emphasis is on the human being and its presumed uniqueness.

If we resort to the two fundamental dimensions of man mentioned by Mircea Eliade (the sacred and the profane), then the historical being demands a man divided between the temptation of the mythical time and the end of the historical time in which he creates and *self*-creates[21] (in reality, a pessimistic view would say he loses himself, transferring just a shadow of the transformed historical reality). The modern historical being can only hope to arrive (at the moment when the circle closes) by abandoning its history. Pretentious or not, history is no longer a beneficial circularity for the modern man and it has become an evil imprisonment where he can no longer regain his essence.

The schematism of circularity

It seems circularity involves a schematic way of thinking (within the boundaries of a straightforward discourse, unbothered by contradictory and unmodifiable interruptions) which justifies a theoretical sufficiency meant to start us thinking. There is too much "settling" and argumentative stability, as well as a deliberate balance which excludes dynamism – something that can come off as a decline. The point we are trying to prove in this paper is

---

[19] Ibid., p. 37.

[20] I have discovered the importance of circularity (its methodological value) in science in general and for philosophy in particular while reading the works of Alexandru Surdu from the volume *Vocaţii filosofice româneşti.* (Philosophical Romanian Vocations). This concept (and its principal value) has also been revealed by *Constantin Noica and the question about the human being.* Other works: *Întrebarea cu trei introduceri la Constantin Noica* (The question with three introductions in Constantin Noica), *Semnificaţia psihologiei consonantiste* (The significance of consonant psichology by Ştefan Odobleja), *Marele proiect al lui Ştefan Odobleja* (The big project by Ştefan Odobleja) and, finnaly, the work that influenced the title of this chapter, *Tema circularităţii* (The circularity notion) *by D. Danielopolu, Şt. Odobleja, P. Postelnicu and C. Noica.*

[21] Mircea Eliade, *The Myth of the Eternal Return,* translated from the French by Willard R. Trask (New York: Harper & Brothers Publishers, 1959), pp. VII–VIII.

quite the opposite: all the stages surpassed in a circle do not represent a paradox nor hasty generality capable of illicitly revisiting the arguments of any experience.

In order to avoid the vicious circularity, we need to start from the universal circle of the being, the Parmenidean circle, and then add the ontological constructions formulated by the classical history of philosophy, from Plato and Aristotle, up to Hegel and Kant. Hegel's way of asking questions about the being always references the unique being – immobile, impenetrable – which, even when confronted with its becoming within thinking and even after the becoming itself, remains the starting point. For Hegel, the idea passes through the world but remains with the self (enriched through becoming). For Kant, the passing is already determined (standardized) by the nuances of thought identified with the being. However, the being and the becoming are still on opposite ends, so we should conceive them not in a linear opposition, having contrasting meanings, but in a circular opposition – the positive builds on the negative and the other way around. From this perspective, the becoming should not oppose the being – if we consider it the mean, the vehicle - but it opposes *reasoning* because this is precisely what makes the transition possible; it introduces and, at the same time, enlightens us inside the "logical jungle".[22]

It is necessary for reasoning to close the circle and escape the "unilateral contradiction" because this is the only way it can identify with the being. The becoming contradicts the being but still waits for it and even tries to meet it, yet the being is one looking for becoming.

> The most important path for this "escape", where distancing yourself from the being is getting you closer is *the circle* – the image of becoming within being. We are therefore talking about a different dialectic from that of Hegel. Noica believes that the origin of this dialectic can be traced down to Kant's table of categories. [23]

Alexandru Surdu retrieves the issue of circularity, and it becomes the methodological principle for sciences and philosophy (Ştefan Odobleja, Paul Postelnicu, Daniel Danielopolu şi Constantin Noica). The following list of terms attributed to this issue coincides in meaning up to a certain point, and they can be used in medicine, psychology, engineering, and philosophy, 'enabling the output of works that will later be seen as fundamental in their fields, at least from a Romanian perspective.'[24] The terms allow the

---

[22] Constantin Noica, *Trei introduceri la devenirea întru fiinţă,* 1984, p. 55.
[23] Alexandru Surdu, *Vocaţii filosofice româneşti* (Romanian philosophical vocations), (Bucharest: The Romanian Academy Publishing, 1995), p. 90.
[24] Ibid., p. 132.

description of phenomena set in different types of relations: coordination, subordination or supra-ranking (in sciences), which later have been conceptualized in the Western literature as well. [25] We can call it 'balanced reflex circle', 'deficit balanced reflex circle', 'vicious reflex circle' (Danielopolu), 'vicious circle' (Postelnicu) or 'vicious circle' that reproduces the 'circularity scheme' *(feedback)* 'with philosophical, moral, logical and pedagogical general implications' (Odobleja). But the general methodological significance surpasses the strict fields to which they are applied, becoming, thanks to Constantin Noica, a scheme of actual thinking, a central philosophical matter.[26]

Models of circularity

The models of circularity have often gotten invoked throughout the history of philosophy, either as the image of a circle – one which represents stability and unity due to the economy of the shape and the balance of the distances that relate to the centre – or the image of a curve (especially in science), an ellipse or a hyperbola, all able to describe laws, phenomena and periodical moves with some accurately conceived amplitudes. In the physical, chemical, biological, social and psychological world of phenomena, there are moments of relative balance represented as periodical ascensions or decreases, which intervene in the mutual rapports between the vectors combined to represent a repetitive process. When this occurs, the theoretical constructs that describe the rapports gain a wave-like trait. The model for these precise phenomena has a dynamic shape which also considers the time factor.

The circle is the image of perfection. The curve is its partial image, decomposed in space and time, where these relations between phenomena or their characteristics that have particular reproductive stability and mutually stimulate become representations of evolution. The evolutionary trait of some processes involves a contradictory aspect, with maximums and minimums, augmentations and decreases that keep repeating themselves until the inner energies get spent. The image of the curve is very important

---

[25] To get the philosophical meaning of circularity, see Friedrich Kümmel, *Platon und Hegel zur ontologischen Begründung des Zirkels in der Erkenntnis*, Tübingen, 1968, or Wiener's cybernetics from 1948; But Danielopolu has been configuring his perception of the reflex vicious circle since 1923, applied for the gastric tabetic crisis, while in *Psihologia consonantistă* (Consonant Psychology) by Ştefan Odobleja, from 1938, „the notion of vicious circle is positively applied in all sciences" – see Alexandru Surdu, *Vocaţii filosofice româneşti*, 1995, pp. 136–137.
[26] Ibid., pp. 132–135.

in biology, psychology and social studies. The model of the curve and that of the circle make a comeback in physics, mechanics, chemistry and the sciences of informatics. The circle is a projection of the sphere, the image of perfection, of Reason's supremacy, of Thought's universality, duplicated by the image of the Cosmos.

As a paradigm with an extended theoretical value (where we also include the negative meaning – the negativity of the 'vicious circle' has always been placed before the positivity and the creative affirmation within a real dialectic, which 'regains' the becoming within being, for example, in Noica's case), circularity has been around, historically speaking, ever since ancient times. But as a model and a principle for the sciences and philosophy, we could say that circularity has been approached of late, starting with the past century, when its positive significance got discovered, along with its normative, methodological and theoretical value.

Circular becoming – mythos and logos

We intend to bring those traits of the circularity expressed historically down to a few fundamental elements, proper to the context in which the ideas have been expressed and to the forms that have emerged, among which some have a specific cultural way of becoming. Out of all the possible examples we could mention afterwards *in extenso* to serve a general synthesis, we will choose two theoretical situations of different complexity, one from Plato *(Statesman)* and the other from Noica.

For Plato,[27] the Universe complies with a duality. It also participates in the divine (circular) motion, 'when it is left undisturbed and when the revolutions have completed its rightful measure of time.' Moreover, by leaving the sacred order, it also takes part in the corporality of the material world; this is when its movement changes course towards the opposite direction. By escaping the divine, it enters the material world, the ever-changing corporal, and travels on its own. This change is seen as an abandonment (absence) of the divine:

> From all of these considerations, it follows that one must neither say that the cosmos is always itself responsible for its turning, nor say at all that it is turned by god in a pair of opposed revolutions, nor again that it is turned by some pair of gods whose thoughts are opposed to each other; it is rather what

---

[27] Plato, *Statesman,* translated by C.J. Rowe, in *idem, Complete Works,* edited, with Introduction and Notes, by John M. Cooper, associate editor D.S. Hutchinson (Indianapolis/Cambridge: Hacket Publishing Company, 1997), pp. 310–317 (269 c-275 b).

was said just now, which is the sole remaining possibility, that at times it is helped by the guidance of another, divine, cause, acquiring life once more and receiving a restored immortality from its craftsman, while at other times, when it is let go, it goes on its own way under its own power, having been let go at such a time as to travel backwards for many tens of thousands of revolutions because of the very fact that its movement combines the effects of its huge size, perfect balance, and its resting on the smallest of bases. [28]

It requires mentioning that the movement (the becoming) must undergo a 'transcendent censorship' directed towards another meaning of the becoming, a negative, even destructive one. Divinity (the eternal divine shepherd) allows things to move according to their nature. Paradoxically, the profane becoming, opposite to the one belonging to the sacred, is a reflection in a type of mirror which distorts reality, as if polarities would absolutely change inside the structure (both physically and psychologically): the old tends to become new again and the organic matter, subject to the passing of time, instead of disintegrating and re-entering the cycle of life (getting old, dying), it gets 'reabsorbed' by the same circuit, passing through the same stages, but reversed. Even so, the Universe travels (becomes) *on its own* and in the opposite direction.

> First, the visible age of every creature, whatever it was, stopped increasing, and everything mortal ceased moving in the direction of looking older; instead, it changed back in the opposite direction, and grew as it were younger, more tender. [29]

Old people become children, and youngsters go back to being newborns. The changes are both physical and psychological.

By using the voice of the Stranger, Plato introduces a myth into this dialogue, reproducing a logical and an ontic paradox (the negative of the universal movement destroys the good governance – positivity of the dynamics and chronology established by the Demiurge). The sentences lose their descriptive value – theoretical – offered by logos, and they become anti-sentences: 'The man grows old' is a sentence that no longer has a meaning; concerning the general, 'the logos' is confused, so the affirmation becomes a negation. Even though we are tempted to understand this myth as a digression meant to amplify the dramatic 'tension' of the dialogue, it does play quite a considerable role in the inner logic of the text, especially if we were to relate it to what commentators have to say about the value of Plato's mythological thinking. We believe that it means to emphasize once

---

[28] Ibid., 270 a.
[29] Ibid., 270 d-e.

again the purpose of the method, of the dialectics and its synthetic superiority, able to draw knowledge (in a paradoxical way) from such different topoi. 'Dialectics is more than just the science of ready-made questions and answers (i.e., Socratic maieutics, n.n. – M.P.). It is the science of flawless spontaneity for both the interviewer and the interviewee.'[30]

If Reason offers harmony and predictability inside a universe governed mainly by the eternal (and immutable), then referencing it – the universal logic – no longer makes sense once the order falls apart: the ontic meaning is thus overturned. The influence of both worlds, by a sort of mythological 'contagion' (which we still do not call reminiscence because it is dialectically valid in the positive Universe), is made possible due to their temporal 'vicinity', even though the myth has an atemporal perspective.

> Clearly, Socrates, reproduction from one another was not part of the nature of things then. It was the earth-born race, the one said to have existed once, that existed then, returning to life again from the earth; it was remembered by our first ancestors, who lived in the succeeding time but bordered on the ending of the previous period, growing up at the beginning of this one. They became our messengers for the accounts of the earth-born, which are nowadays wrongly disbelieved by many people. [31]

However, Plato does not render the myth comprehensible because otherwise, he would create an imbalance between logos and mythos. Still, we cannot help ourselves but compare this myth (whose relevance surpasses the mythological) with the cosmological model of the expanding Universe – described with the help of quantum physics – which pulsates just as contradictory between the *Big Bang* and the *Big Crunch*. Should we also turn this theory into a mythological perspective that neither common (modern) sense nor reason can grasp? Could it be possible that things cannot be described (imagined) both ways – platonic and current – by the same dialectics of the mythos-logos 'contamination'? Or, on the contrary, the paradox of moving against time has its well-established theoretical purpose since mythos and logos interpenetrate in both situations? Contrary circular meanings are being proposed there and here as well. Here and beyond, the singularity of universes baffles Reason, but this does not mean that the proposed models do not come from a logical construction (logical mathematics, by Einstein's theory, at least), which is still *inconceivable*, at least for common sense. John Barrow was saying related to this that

---

[30] Constantin Noica, *Schiță pentru istoria lui Cum e cu putință ceva nou* (A Sketch for the history of How is something new possible), (Bucharest: Humanitas Publishing, 1995), p. 50.
[31] Plato, *Statesman,* 1997, 271 a-b.

the answer to this dilemma is to give up on the classical notion of singularity as a place with infinite temperature and density. Instead, we can say that a singularity appears when each ray of the sun passing through time and space stops and it is no longer able to continue. What can be any more «singular» than this experience similar to that of Alice in Wonderland? At the end of its road, the ray of light reached the end of space and time. It "disappears" from the Universe.[32]

That is how circularity brings the visible Universe together with the thought Universe, the rational one, gathering space and time (sometimes a reversed space and time) into a whole. This unity obliterates the logic of reality but not of the being. The journey of both models (Plato's and that of the *Big Bang*) imply a becoming, an expansion and confinement, no matter if we call it circular or consider it inside a circularity that sums both positivity and negativity at the same time. On both ends, the being closes/opens the cycle. The paradox of becoming itself (the tension between mythos and logos) is like matter passing into anti-matter or the concentration of the actual Universe into a three millimetres sphere at just one-thousandth of a second after the grand explosion. The significance of this sentence, right here, right now, is it not overlapping another, uttered more than two thousand years ago: 'We must suppose that this change is, of the turnings that occur in the heavens, the greatest and the most complete turning of all.'?[33]

As a last resort, however, it is not its cosmological unexperienced significance we are interested in, nor the metaphysical one, but the historical, which achieves the humane universal, even if it is paradoxically:

If old men went back to being children, it follows that people should be put together again from the dead, there in the earth, and come back to life; they would be following the reversal of things, with coming into being turning round with it to the opposite direction, and since they would according to this argument necessarily come into existence as earth-born, they would thus acquire that name and have that account given of them– all those of them, that is, whom god did not take off to another destiny. [34]

But for Plato, circularity has mainly a dialectical meaning. His discourse is not *aiming* at describing one impression of the contradictory-becoming Universe but at attaining the concept – in case it arises interest, the

---

[32] John D. Barrow, *Originea Universului* (The Origin of the Universe), (Bucharest: Humanitas Publishing, 1994), p. 52.
[33] Plato, *Statesman,* 1997, 270 c.
[34] Ibid., 271 b-c.

statesman. That is the stake of one reasoning able to create a space – logical – for the concept through consecutive restrains. In this area of the connections built through logic ('our thinking got away intact'), the thesis applies to almost any dialogue. Logos references the humane, whose order it imposes and establishes as a unique measure: in the case of the *Sophist,* the 'existence of the non-existent was enforced'; in defining the statesman, dialectics is the compromise – the regal way – to convince the others:

> But it is not painting or any other sort of manual craft, but speech and discourse, that constitute the more fitting medium for exhibiting all living things, for those who are able to follow; for the rest, it will be through manual crafts. [35]

Each one of his dialogues follows one way or another the same circular path: the proposition of a concept (the definition) delays it into the most diverse areas (sometimes contradictory) of reality, which he divides by genres until it reaches the proper one where we will find it in the end.

The same happens in *Politikos.* We are advised not to deviate from the road that gets us closer to the purpose of the journey: clearly defining the concept of the statesman. Our excursion through myth is not some stylistic or literary delay but a model, a way to gradually get closer to the main reason (the politic) through dialectics. But how does one advance towards the goal by seemingly moving away and setting *history* within brackets while still retelling it in mythological terms? In reality, we are not dealing with alienation but with a return (a circular regaining of the authentic human being that has gone through the history of 'it was meant to be') of the divine essence from inside man and the sacrament of the polis. That happens because ancestors directed the regular return. History endures a distortion inside the great myths of humanity, and it always gets pushed towards the future. We can recover history through archetypes – which *reveal* themselves to man – connect it to the great eras and the golden ages. As a result, time gains a certain circularity by engaging history as well. The image itself suddenly becomes much more familiar considering the same paradox of the historical passing (becoming) – as familiar as the ways of referencing the 'sub-quantic' reality described by microphysics can be. One cannot express historical time without the contribution of the fourth dimension – time. The present time of every society bends along the sacred reality of archetypes. The relation between space and time references the archetype as a centre from which it cannot escape. 'Basically, the horizon of archetypes and repetition cannot be transcended with impunity unless we

---

[35] Ibid., 277 c.

accept a philosophy of freedom that does not exclude God.'[36] Exactly what Eliade formulates in a paradigmatic way, following the logic of the 'Great Time' of cosmic cycles, it becomes the image of the invincible logos in Plato that periodically commands order from the universal movement. Therefore, inside the myth described in *Politikos*, the recurrent withdrawal of the divine Shepard is counterbalanced by the recurrent comeback of the divine order, placing the values of the organised cosmos above everything. The divine centre – the centre of the rational Universe – coordinates this organised cosmos. The corporal and the negative chaotic movement (in opposite directions) means havoc above all, but any havoc requires the restoration of the order it references. This reference is circular. Order is restored, it is logos, classification according to gender, and the rigour of concept. Two contradictory tendencies periodically traverse the Universe. If the circuit gains a contrary meaning (negative), everything falls apart, corrupted in its being. The logos is no longer the defeater: '[...] the cause of this was the bodily element in its mixture (of the universe – n. M.P.), its companion since its origins long in the past because this element was marked by a great disorder before it entered into the present world-order.'[37] The risk of persevering inside the world of corporal movement and of the chaos this has caused is that the experience of disorder (which is old and imprinted in its structure) tends to destroy it. The entropy disintegrates genres, logic, and laws and determines 'its own sinking into the bottomless sea of dissimilarity'. The reign of the Good is not even reminiscent anymore. Humanity, as a gender, shrinks, becomes distorted, becomes primary rank biology, and it resorbs itself inside the mineral from where it comes back, just like a spontaneous generation. Similar to dissolution, returning to order is still at the mercy of the Divine that, by reinstalling the good it interrupts this era of disintegration. Circularity inside the myth is the theme of contradiction. The disposition of the cosmic cycle also includes history, even though it is not looking to impose it as a theme but to include it in the repetition (and regeneration at the same time) of the cosmos. The myth of eternal repetition means a supreme attempt to 'transfix' becoming:

> If all moments and all situations of the cosmos are repeated ad ifinitum, their evanescence is patent in the last analysis; sub specie infimtatis, all moments and all situations remain stationary and thus acquire the ontological order of the archetype. Hence, among all the forms of becoming, historical becoming too is saturated with being. From the point of view of eternal repetition,

---

[36] M. Eliade, *The Myth of the Eternal Return,* 1959, p. 160.

[37] Plato, *Statesman,* 1997, p. 315 (273 b).

historical events are transformed into categories, thus regaining the ontological order they possessed on the horizon of archaic spirituality. [38]

Therefore, concerning Plato, we can assume a certain circularity, firstly in the logical way of building the concept (here we are talking about the 'stateman') through dialectics and the two contradictory ways – *diaeresis* and *synagogue* – and secondly in the ontological relation between mythos and logos. Regarding Noica, on the same theme but related to the being, this becomes a major issue in philosophy. We might even dare say a fundamental one. Moreover, he sets becoming in direct connection to the being, and history (a particular case of becoming – the historical becoming) is the starting point for his discourse on modern times. Every great philosophical theme begins with a 'logical chaos', then comes around the need for 'a real dialogue, some effective contradictions or a determined chaos'.[39] The fact that dialectics allows us to 'pin down' the logical reference points of the being, which is no longer hiding inside an untouchable kingdom since it receives (and imprints) reality, even the historical one, is also due to the becoming. Its positive logical form taken into consideration by the knowledgeable subject is becoming within being.

By weaving together the characteristics of the ancient ontology of substantialism – brought into discussion by medieval nominalism ('through nominalism emerges the idea of an absolute separation between the ontic reality and the humane knowledge'[40]), Noica must notice the universal 'disarray' of things, the permanent snap in reality's balance and the real constructive opposition of concept, which evolves into a dialectics 'of circles'. 'Passing from one dialectical circle to another is done by transforming the notion of "theme" from the first circle into an "anti-theme" in the second one'[41] but not by using a synthesis of contradictions or a quiet resolved and irreducible balance inside a Hegelian identity. That gets done by finding a meaning, which will finally become the meaning of becoming, or as Noica put it, 'the circular dialectics that has a direction and it is *oriented.*'[42]

---

[38] M. Eliade, *The Myth of the Eternal Return,* 1959, p. 123.
[39] C. Noica, *Trei introduceri la devenirea întru ființă,* 1984, p. 56.
[40] Claudiu Baciu, *Perspectiva funcționalistă a ontologiei lui Noica* (Noica's ontology and its functional perspective), in *Studii de istorie a filosofiei românești* (Studies on the history of Romanian philosophy), vol. II, coord. by Viorel Cernica (Bucharest: Publishing House of the Romanian Academy, 2007), p. 339.
[41] Al. Surdu, *Vocații filosofice românești*, 1995, p. 136.
[42] Ibid.

Philosophical consciousness starts from dialogue and becomes possible thanks to the necessity of connecting contradictory elements. It also brings on irrationality. According to Noica, this irrationality emerges from consciousness, and it is *a particular* type of irrationality, not a total logical chaos but one that precedes it and has to be considered the starting point through dialogue – therefore, the dialogue *is real.* According to Plato, dialogue and logos are not determined by the irrational: 'Platonism seemed to have the freedom to start anywhere – since it already had from the beginning, within the Idea, the congruence of reality, any reality, with the essential…' [43] However, the dialogue stands at the core of reality, but it is the logos which wraps and unwraps everything at the same time together with dialectics. They do so by separating and uniting the elements, by circularly separating and combining them, while the concept remains the core of this circularity, a method used in *Politikos* as well. [44]

The becoming – including the historical one – brings the issue of the being into the real, continuously changing the world, and still manages to overcome this transformation (becoming for becoming) because the being precedes it. If we were to remain on the level of Creation – history's irrational 'in which philosophy truly submerges nowadays' [45] – we would neither have circularity (the appropriate road for becoming, philosophy or the dialectics of circles) nor history. History does not move forward towards itself and does not persist as irrational concerning the being. By overcoming this chaos with the help of philosophy, history gains access to the being and evolves into becoming within the being.

If we gradually follow Noica's string of dialectics, we notice the strictness with which the concept of historical trait 'questions' its philosophy. Not so much the philosophy of history as part of the discourse, but more like philosophy in general. In reality, philosophy cannot escape genres. It is not an evasion of what could be understood as a metaphysics of history (it is a contradiction of terms, but it is still possible as a project, just as Kant envisioned it, a metaphysics of physics [46]), but rather a focus on the becoming, using the traditional conceptual mechanism of science, as well as the modern one. It first comes across becoming as history by forging a critique of the possibility of history through self-reflection. Kant elaborated a critique of physics while searching for metaphysics and returned to physics in the same (vicious?) spot of his philosophical search.

---

[43] C. Noica, *Trei introduceri la devenirea întru ființă*, 1984, p. 56.
[44] David A. White, *Myth, Metaphysics and Dialectic in Plato's Statesman* (Ashgate Publishing, Ltd., 2007), p. 6.
[45] C. Noica, *Trei introduceri la devenirea întru ființă*, 1984, p. 74.
[46] Ibid., p. 61.

The same did, says Noica, maybe, Descartes and Leibniz, ending up
envisioning the *Mathesis universalis*, in the case of the first one, and the
second in *Scientia generalis* when they would not end up in particular
sciences. [47]

The fundamental obsession of philosophy that has persisted throughout
history aims at the being, counterbalanced by questions about the spirit, and
translated into the relationship between *what is* and *how is it possible* what
it is. The first has been identified, according to Noica, as the being (the
substance), and it ends up in the transcendent, while the other has been
identified as *becoming* and it ends up in the transcendental. The Ideal, the
golden cut, able to reconcile – not reunite, but rather facilitate cohabitation
and self-confirmation – of both the being and the spirit consists in clearly
defining the sphere in which the unity between the transcendent and the
transcendental is possible (and authentic). [48] From before Socrates and up
until Aristotle, the being reclaims itself through a majestic endeavour. But
Aristotle opens a gateway through this monolithic – and sometimes
redundant – affirmation of the being without annulling the fundamental
unity while still allowing the individual to recommence his ascending
towards the real-world and be the mirror of the universal. 'The issue of
balance between the individual being and the general essence, therefore,
constitutes the core of the Aristotelian question' says Noica, quoting a
German source.[49]

So, what true path should philosophy take to reach unity between the being
and the spirit or between the transcendent and the transcendental? Could the
transcendental – which is not proper to Kant, but to Socrates – be its ultimate
target that could recreate the unity between the transcendent and the
transcendental? Since the instant philosophy itself starts to take an interest
in becoming as a reality with a purpose (philosophical), the issue of
congruency between these two fields gains a new perspective inside the
historical becoming – within becoming lay all forms of knowledge. This
one acknowledges the importance of becoming and history's value. Perhaps
it has always been close to the philosophical spirit, but it has also been
systematically assumed by Hegel's philosophy.

Every philosophy has assumed liberty; it has even established it as its
core value, but it ended up pulled outside its sphere and the vivid reality
(that is history) due to an excessive process of becoming abstract. No

---

[47] Ibid.

[48] Ibid., pp. 64–65.

[49] Idem, *Schiță pentru istoria lui Cum e cu putință ceva nou* (A Sketch for the History
of How is something new possible), 1995, p. 107, n. 1.

philosophy can be super-human, not even when wished for, because it needs to begin from the man and account for 'all the dimensions through which man moves […] and brings them closer to the cosmos.' [50]

Liberty (for Noica more than for Hegel, or maybe for Noica but as a follow-up from Kant) has a value *for* human consciousness that stands against (at any cost and with all the arguments of its being projected towards a cultural geometrical ideal) history seen as low becoming or a becoming that does not close the circle of the being in general.

In his work *Mathesis and the simple joys,* he understands history as a necessary evil that needs replacement because it spiritually divides and scatters us into our solitudes, dividing us into units of space and time.[51] Later on, Kant's categories and their schematism applied to the becoming of the spirit reorganizes precisely the category of culture and incorporates it into becoming in general. When history casts its shadow in every corner of culture and increases its questions, it does so not to baffle the subject (the empirical and historical subject) but to stimulate it to retie philosophy's string to follow its positive path. Historical becoming is amplified inside its ontological significance and obtains the positive of the permanent flow while becoming a principle nobody can no longer ignore due to *Tratat de ontologie (Treatise on Ontology).* Initially invalidated, history returns us to the world because it communicates a state of things which we would otherwise overlook. Philosophy refuses to become an ideological appendix, to sustain historicism and relativism, just like it refuses to serve theology or sciences (positivism).

> Philosophy not only has the purpose to pull consciousness out of the irrational of the historical becoming but also to pull itself out of history and historicism. Nowadays, it starts with becoming and introduces reason in the becoming's irrational *to understand and dominate it* (s. n., M. P.), not to get even more lost in it.[52]

At this point, we believe that liberty is related to knowledge, the source where philosophy reclaims an essential role and the freedom *of action* in history, together with the arguments of spirit, not of the historicity, which univocally determines self-conscience – historicism. This liberty of actual historical conditioning of the human being gains the traits of the culture that

---

[50] Mircea Eliade, *Solilocvii* (Soliloquies), (Bucharest: Humanitas Publishing, 1991), p. 20.
[51] C. Noica, *Mathesis sau bucuriile simple* (Mathesis or the Simple Joys), (Bucharest: Fundația pentru Literatură și Artă „Regele Carol al II-lea" Publishing, 1934), p. 18, 19.
[52] N. Noica, *Trei introduceri la devenirea întru ființă*, 1984, pp. 58–59.

assumes history. When history denies knowledge to the freedom of concept by constraining the spirit (free) towards historicism, then it is no longer a form contributing to the creation of the historical being and becomes a restrictive and condemning historicism. It does not deny itself as history, but welcomes it as self-apprehension leads philosophical conscience into rebuilding the connexion between the transcendent (what it is) and the transcendental (how is it possible what it is). The question of historicity is truly a primordial one for humankind and fundamental in philosophy because it is tightly linked with time: our awareness of time cannot become separated from the awareness of living in time, which is history. In reality, Noica does not distract us from history (the concept of pure historical conditioning, understood as becoming within being or becoming within thinking) but wishes to purposefully interrogate the human (a real being able to reason and to think) and his ingoing from the revolving time into the uttering time, the one able to logically build. According to Alexandru Surdu,

> the becoming within being suggests going from individual to general and from concrete to abstract inside the human mind by extending this authentic dialogue of the spirit of Noica's philosophy. The being of the world is thus its own logical image.[53]

The topic of historicity as historicism is the topic of becoming as becoming, where the spirit denies itself the low becoming, the permanent indistinctness, the flowing of nature towards chaos and indetermination. It is a problem that man always has to face in his intention to *make* history and oppose logic and the reality in his thoughts as an expression of inner liberty or the expression of a reality done not for man but for nature (or simply for the becoming as becoming). Turning towards himself saves man in and from history, as well as from the loneliness locally and temporally multiplicated. It brings him through time to a universal specifically humane, a humanity attained (thought) inside a concept. That is how we believe Noica understands the purpose of history regarding becoming.

References

Aron, Raymond. 1997. *Introducere în filosofia istoriei* (Introduction to the Philosophy of History). Bucharest: Humanitas Publishing.
Baciu, Claudiu. 2007. *Perspectiva funcționalistă a ontologiei lui Noica* (Noica's ontology and its functional perspective), in *Studii de istorie a filosofiei românești* (Studies on the history of Romanian philosophy),

---

[53] Al. Surdu, *Vocații filosofice românești*, 1995, p. 97.

vol. II, coord. by Viorel Cernica. Bucharest: Publishing House of the Romanian Academy.

Barrow, John D. 1994. *Originea Universului* (The Origin of the Universe). Bucharest: Humanitas Publishing.

Brandon, Robert N. 1978. *Evolution.* "Philosophie of Science", vol. 45, no. 1 (Mar., 1978).

Eliade, Mircea. 1959. *The Myth of the Eternal Return,* translated from the French by Willard R. Trask. New York: Harper & Brothers Publishers.

Eliade, Mircea. 1991. *Solilocvii* (Soliloquies). Bucharest: Humanitas Publishing.

Noica, Constantin. 1934. *Mathesis sau bucuriile simple* (Mathesis or the simple joys). Bucharest: The Foundation for Literature and Art „Regele Carol al II-lea".

Noica, Constantin. 1984. *Trei introduceri la devenirea întru fiinţă* (Three Introductions to Becoming Within Being). Bucharest: University Publishing.

Noica, Constantin. 1995. *Schiţă pentru istoria lui Cum e cu putinţă ceva nou* (A Sketch for the history of How is something new possible). Bucharest: Humanitas Publishing.

Noica, Constantin. 1995. *Pagini despre sufletul românesc* (Pages on the Romanian Spirit). Bucharest: Humanitas Publishing.

Plato. 1997. *Statesman*, translated by C.J. Rowe, in *idem, Coplete Works,* edited, with Introduction and Notes, by John M. Cooper, associate editor D.S. Hutchinson. Indianapolis/Cambridge: Hacket Publishing Company.

Rădulescu-Motru, Constantin. 2006. *Opere alese* (Selected Works), vol. II, *Vocaţia. Factor hotărâtor în cultura popoarelor. Timp şi destin* (Vocation. Crucial factor in the culture of peoples. Time and destiny). Bucharest: Publishing House of the Romanian Academy.

Surdu, Alexandru. 1995. *Vocaţii filosofice româneşti* (Romanian philosophical vocations). Bucharest: Romanian Academy Publishing.

Van den Berghe, Pierre L. 1990. *Why Mast Sociologists Don't (and Won't) Think Evolutionary,* in „Sociological Forum", vol. 5, no. 2 (Iun., 1990).

White, David A. 2007. *Myth, Metaphysics and Dialectic in Plato's Statesman.* Ashgate Publishing Ltd.

CHAPTER IV

A.D. XENOPOL ON THE PERSPECTIVE OF NOICA'S TWO 'MEASURES' OF PHILOSOPHY

In a text published in the Romanian magazine 'Convorbiri literare' (Literary dialogues)[1] in the year 1944, Constantin Noica says that Romanian philosophy, at least through its most important agents – "from Haşdeu's philosophical flashes, […], continuing with Conta, Xenopol, Pârvan and Motru, up until Blaga" – is, in fact, a construct developed as an extension of our nature, not a rebellious act set in the extension of our thinking, which assumes it as being unnatural, as Greek philosophy does in particular or the western one, in general. For the Western culture, this breach – the consciousness of being sits *before* the world – is natural and beneficial to its pattern of acquiring knowledge that otherwise cannot be conceived. The human detaches himself from the world and looks at it through his alienated being, aware of this alienation from his spirit's height. 'Aware of this fact, he does not just get alienated from the world, but he can also be, in an absurd way, against it.'[2]

Between being aware of the alienation (the breach between mind and work, looking for a *purpose* in the world) and continuing the world through

---

[1] *Cum gândeşte poporul român* (The way of thinking of the Romanian nation), text included in *Pagini despre sufletul românesc* (Pages about the Romanian spirit), The „Luceafărul" Collection, Bucharest, 1944. The studies and the essays included here should have been part of a greater paper, *Contribuţii la o istorie a vieţii spirituale româneşti* (Contribution to a history of the Romanian spiritual life), or as Noica states in the Preface, a history of the Romanian philosophy in fact, ordered by a German publishing house through the Romanian Institute from Berlin. The author thinks that `a history of the Romanian spiritual life` is more suitable in the present cultural (and political) frame, giving us better credit abroad than a history of the Romanian philosophy would, at least for now'. See also the edition with the same title that we are going to use further on, published in Bucharest, Humanitas Publishing House, 1991.

[2] C. Noica, *Pagini despre sufletul românesc* (Pages on the romanian soul), (Bucharest: Humanitas Publishing House, 1991), p. 79.

thought, an area where the Romanian philosophy can also be situated, constantly alluding to the rural wisdom, Noica is searching for those two distinct sensibilities that can generate a philosophy. There are also two measures that match these sensibilities, two ways of thinking about the natural and the unnatural feeling of separating from the world, two ways of philosophically pondering: to nature's extent, making thought in permanent harmony with the world (the Romanian philosophy up until a certain date), or dividing the world from the spirit through the sad realisation of the breach – 'the spirit does not get lost in the world and it does not just extend it',[3] in the case of western philosophy.

By looking at philosophy in general, through these terms – of continuity and discontinuity between the spirit and the world – Noica suggests his own view on the Romanian philosophical 'sensibility'. In fact, he raises the issue of Romanian philosophical thinking, of the ratio between the eternal and the historical or between historical culture and geometrical culture, and even the relation between knowledge and Romanian philosophy's affinity for the greater fields of classical philosophy. He does so in the before-mentioned work, but also in others, starting perhaps from his first book, *Mathesis sau bucuriile simple (Mathesis or the simple joys),* in general, not according to the Romanian spiritual sensibility. In this first book, for example, he highly praises *forgetfulness* (a particular type of forgetfulness, able to pull us out of history, the ephemeral) as spiritual therapy meant to cure us of the illness of history that drives the contemporary human to wish not to abandon anything from 'all of his and the world's sins'.[4] This contemporary human wears the stigmata of history, able to read himself just like a book, from left to right, as an endless string of events and not as an opposition or a forever-rebellious startle (historical as well, we must admit) against history and the being. Thus, Noica's commandment 'Rid yourselves of history!' Reading and refining the tension of this attitude become deeply human (and philosophical): reason turns against nature (of man and the world), looking for a meaning, not a lesson. And to be able to find a meaning, one must abandon all possible meanings, as well as the hermeneutics of historical signs, which one can escape just by forgetting everything and relating to a singular thing: 'Let's stop any movement, let's omit everything and sleep our general sleep – and then dream.'[5] To dream here means to forget oneself in the world and enter the spiritual realm to acquire a historical sensibility, described as a rational measure and being, in fact, a lack of measure (excess of rationality).

---

[3] Ibid.
[4] Idem, *Mathesis sau bucuriile simple* (Mathesis or the simple joys), (Bucharest: Humanitas Publishing House, 1992), p. 37.
[5] Ibid., p. 44.

This excess – against the existence and the ability to pull conscience out of the natural course of things (the cosmos) – does not occur, according to Noica, in the history of the Romanian people. The dimension of Romanian philosophy stands calm and steady behind things and objects, like an extension of them in our conscience, hardly willing to doubtfully vibrate but rather contemplate and spiritually replenish the state of the being inside which it established itself. In a previous text that opens with a quote by Cioran,[6] Noica retraces the journey of our spiritual history by focusing on the tension between the eternal and the historical from three perspectives. He chooses three great personalities as reference points of thought and spiritual relation to the world: Neagoe Basarab, Dimitrie Cantemir and Lucian Blaga.

The moment from the year 1520, rendered by *Învăţăturile lui Neagoe Basarab către fiul său Teodosie (The teachings of Neagoe Basarab for his son Teodosie)* perfectly fits eternity through contemplation, repressing personal urge (by lack of personality) and the impulse to confirm and merge with the realm of creation, says Noica. The conscience saves itself in eternity by praising God and ignoring oneself. Therefore, no scientific curiosity can emerge from this, but the human can only be interested in a path that throws him out of the world and towards an unhistorical bliss.

> No doubt, philosophy is lost, says Noica, the conscious contact with the world, the source of knowledge and moral behaviour, the intimate root of will.[7]

We can distinguish in Dimitrie Cantemir's works, almost two centuries later, the wish for history and the moral reorganisation of the community he is a part of, as well as the people he represents and leads. For him, criticising the historical and moral faults (balanced by their noble origin or the more elevated traits, like courage in battle) represents an opportunity for an authentic ethical imputation addressed to the Romanian people. This attitude from *Descriptio Moldaviae* must not be interpreted as an excess of objectiveness or historical criticism meant to arouse a national ideal, but rather this leader's refusal, also as a European man of culture to allow himself to be seduced by the mental predispositions of his people, leaning not towards making history, but towards assuming it as a fatality. Cantemir does not judge his people by the standards of his own spiritual and historical evolution, even though he sometimes exaggerates its defects – 'arrogance

---

[6] C. Noica, *Ce e etern şi ce e istoric în cultura românească* (What is eternal and what is historical in Romanian culture), in *Pagini despre sufletul românesc*, 1991, p. 6.
[7] Ibid., p. 17./3

and pride; bickering attitude but also exceeding conciliation; [...] inconsistency, sometimes an extremely dynamic spirit and other times extremely mild and soft'. Moreover, he considers they have a consistent lack of interest in high culture ('they believe educated men lose their mind') and judges them[8] by the moral standards and ethical categories of Western culture. By criticising his people because they do not rise to the proper historical forms, nor they oppose the categories of spirit to the ancestral patterns that make them prone to laziness and cultural languishment, the bright ruler, author of *Istoria Imperiului Otoman (The History of the Ottoman Empire),* escapes the unhistorical frame and propels the national ideal into the great culture. Even though most of the criteria he uses to judge the mentality and the nature of Romanian people are not objective, but borrowed from the Western side, his project does not evade the local functional patterns, which the scholar trust in, but aims at a new cultural, spiritual and historical configuration, towards which the nation already aspires in his opinion.

In the case of Lucian Blaga, Noica says that our spirituality, unloaded from the ancestral contemplation to historical criticism, gains a new dimension as it establishes, through the philosophy of stylistic apriorism, a dialogue with the great European philosophies. Does Blaga, though, secure the second dimension (measure) of philosophy, specifically Western? Yes, and no. By trying to restore "Kant's set of categories" and add some categories extracted from areas of the consciousness less explored (mystery), or just because he distinguishes a stylistic hall-mark in any field of culture, linking two worlds "apparently contrasting: the Kantian apriorism and the relativism of the culture's philosophy",[9] the author of *Trilogia culturii (The Trilogy of Culture)* writes philosophy in a Western way. Actually, the endemic and what is outside of history get through as well. We can even say, together with Noica and judging from the originality and the impressive architecture of Blaga's system, that there are elements able to connect us with the most personal systems of Western thought: "With Lucian Blaga, the Romanian spirit exults in philosophy."[10]

As for Noica's ideas on the theory of history, just as we encounter the theory in Xenopol, we believe there are at least three reasons that determine us not to include it in that category of philosophy as an extension of our nature into the spirit. *The first* reason references the opposition: historicity (becoming) and nature. This opposition does not render void the domain of one in favour of the other. For instance, the world understood as becoming

---

[8] Ibid., p. 25.
[9] Ibid., p. 29.
[10] Ibid., p. 91

or as continuous historicity does not exclude the world of repetition, as a pre-existent nature and also as a permanence, but it can rebuild the latter in the light of its own becoming, which leads to knowledge; it is the becoming of the spirit understood as culture. Xenopol sees history as a way of being, and therefore a manner of acquiring knowledge different from the one proposed by the sciences of the universal and opposed to it. History does not negate nature since nature is *also* historical – geology, astronomy, and cosmology, all fall under history in a certain way of looking at things.

The second reason references the distinction between natural regularity and regularity within history. This regularity is particular to nature (which represents the repetition and the consistency of conditions) by definition, and it situates us in a certain way of looking at and knowing things (knowledge is universal) in their relations with the particular.

There are also laws in history, but in different forms, which makes us conclude that the formula of the causative law (proper to sequence, in Xenopol's view) is the second reason for the nature-history/being-spirit breach. The universality of law results in continuance, uniformity and permanence in nature as long as the conditions remain the same. In history, however, the law (the general laws of history, says Xenopol) is present due to the potential (the power) it offers to change, the process and the tendency to develop. There is no permanence or universality in history, other than the measure in which the historical law offers a path towards development. This law Xenopol mentions is universal[11] on the level of humanity but particular on the level of society (community). For example, revolution as such is universal with respect to the entire humanity but particular with respect to the conditions in which it takes place in a certain society (The French Revolution, The 1848 Revolution, and so on).

The historical set is the equivalent of the law in nature. First, it represents permanence and direction (through the ascending sign of time – prediction)

---

[11] Xenopol conceives the individual in a direct relation with the historical general that gets established inside the historical fact. "*We* are using the notion *universal* preferably for that of general, in order to describe phenomena that take place anytime and anywhere. The notion *general* is reserved for phenomena harder to understand and that, even though they do not possess a singular character, they also do not have value anytime and anywhere. This innovative use of terms is a must because history or succession can also formulate *general truths but with an individual character,* not universal, meaning *truths that reach a certain degree of abstraction without actually becoming universal because of this.* Thus, we oppose the notion of *singular* to that of *general* and the notion of *individual* to that of *universal.*" A.D. Xenopol, *Principiile fundamentale ale istoriei* (The Fundamental Principles of History), translated into Romanian from French, introductive study and selected bibliography by Rodica Croitoru (Bucharest: Albatros, 2003), p. 46, note 20.

but also as a way to know and explain the past (descendent, inside the genealogy of the event). Secondly, aren't we opposing nature's spirit (the set) and making history *against nature?* According to Noica, history is a system for Xenopol, a Romanian philosophy: it is the opposition between spirit/nature, a way of being (of telling stories equal to the action of knowing), and it does not come as an extension of human nature since it rebuilds it – a rebuilt made possible through the law of history.

The third reason why Xenopol decided not to align with Noica's category of making philosophy in accordance with human nature is precisely the historical way of being (within history), understood as *the fact of being inside history.*

Xenopol states that science is authentic. Science is not just the product of conscience but also the relation between concepts produced by the spirit, 'the intellectual reproduction of the Universe; it is the reflex of reality into the intellect; *the reason of things projecting itself into human reason*'[12] (emphasis added, M.P.). When we examine these statements, we can see that the discussion of the relationship between the world and the spirit, particularly from a scientific realist perspective, supports Noica's assertion that Xenopol's work is systematic and adds value to a set of original categories. These categories are developed through dialogue (and sometimes opposition) with other philosophical frameworks such as Kant's categorical schematism, Hegel's philosophy, German neo-Kantianism, and French positivism. His philosophy is in opposition to human nature (nature). Scientific realism is a convenient measure of this system to build the terminological and categorical tools directly linked to the phenomenon, experience and pulse of life. The latter determines the structure and how the world and the Universe are reflected by the spirit. This reflection occurs in one direction: the spirit reflects the world and mirrors reality. Science is objective, as it forms inside the object, but its reality is not given in the conscience, nor established in a Kantian way, a priori. Therefore, the law gets constructed starting with the phenomenon, the experience (experiment) and the generalisation; it takes its elements from the described reality reflected into science. The law confirms repetition, and the distance between cause and effect found in the relation between force and conditions gets almost suppressed. In nature, the law is entirely described by *how*, not by a metaphysical construction, by *why* it exists what it already exists. The law is universal in time and space.[13] When Xenopol attempts to propose a system of principles for history, he brings forward the set which acts as law.

---

[12] Ibid., p. 66.
[13] Ibid., p. 94

We must keep in mind that the set is a *sui-generis* concept emerging from the opposition with the notion of repetitive causality, which refers to nature. The set organises not only the history of culture and civilisation but also that of the Universe.

The difference between the two-causality type, that of nature and that of history seems to be a methodological breach. The sets are ways to describe the development and becoming within history, and above all, they are causative sets, while the laws only show us how, and they do not explain why phenomena and processes are the way they are.[14]

To understand the attributes of the set and the way successive causality works, without elaborating on Xenopol's entire system of reasoning, we must still briefly compare the law and the set. Xenopol says that it represents in history what law does in nature. Are the two categories opposed? Are they describing relations or making possible an explanation (an understanding) of the phenomena without resorting to identical cognitive faculties? The difference between them relies on their relationship with time. The law is universal in time but not in space. So, regarding space, there can be exceptions from the law – all the planets of the solar system comply with the gravitational force, but space and other forces (acceleration, the particular dynamic of objects etc.) have their traits, according to ellipses, an inclination of axis and so on – but where time is concerned, there is no exception. Therefore, says Xenopol, on the axis of time, the law is universal: because the conditions are the same, the rapports are permanent ($e = mc^2$, a constant rapport that stays like that throughout the entire known Universe, as long as it exists). The law does not explain (like only the cause can) but describes the way it manifests that which exists:

> The explanation, in all of these cases, is apparent because the law of manifestation is nothing but the pervading phenomenon, which would

---

[14] The Difference between the two ways of being (historical and natural, successive and repetitive) allows Xenopol to introduce the principles of historical knowledge and to establish history as a science. Sometimes, though, he expands the history set to the level of universal development, considering there is a connection between recent historical events, like the foreign dynasty brought to power by those who forced Cuza to abdicate, with events that took place further in the past, like the Romans conquering Dacia or life emerging on planet Earth. Obviously, the sequence set might not always be rigorously established, but the intention of a new methodology (history), alongside a new logic, used only for scientific purposes and not out of needless systematically reasons, is the measure of belief, an authentic thinker and an honest scientist.

conclude that explaining the phenomenon through law will be explaining *the phenomenon through phenomenon,* which is absurd.[15]

Therefore, the explanation is not possible through the law, but it is possible through cause. Cause and law are not identical, although, in other words, if we try to establish the genesis (the why) of an event in the repetitive phenomena (non-historical), we will rapidly approach the ultimate cause. In the case of sequence relation, described by the set, we need to follow the string of causes – the conditions are always different, and the string set comes bearing all the precedents, individual along time and non-recurring. If only one link would break, we would not have a sequence, causality or development, and we would not be in history.

The set is individual in time and universal in space. There is no opposition between law and set, at least not regarding their practicability – nature (repetition) for law and history (succession) for set – as long as nature gets perceived as succession and history as repetition or permanence through the elements that are its agents: the human beings, considered to be biological entities. There are, thou, an essential methodological opposition and a logical one.

In Noica's words:

Any philosophy is also a recovery, not just a recording of the world [...]. Thus, any philosophy is *practically* an excess. The Greeks did not shy away from going all the way until surplus. German Idealism did the same. And these are the two great philosophies of history.[16]

How can we define excess if not as a hypertrophy of a faculty that brings into the equation the entire universe employing one single explanatory stake, rationality? Authentic philosophy is an excess of rationality, a recovery of the world based on a principle that emerges from the spirit, thus a rational principle. The entire effort from the first chapters of *Principiilor fundamentale ale istoriei (The Fundamental Principles of History),* where Xenopol sets up the method and the principles of historical causality, happens to make visible the historical rationality. He finds within the set an equivalent of nature's law. To also give it logical support (the set determines the individual followed in time to enter the historical general – the social one, where actions influence the social life as a whole), he builds a system of categories (historical succession, causality in succession and causality in repetition, the law of repetition and law of succession, action within history

---

[15] Ibid., p. 78.
[16] C. Noica, *Pagini despre sufletul românesc,* 1991, p. 80.

and evolution within history, the law of evolution etc.) meant to impose the historical way of being into the universal. The principles of history become universal principles so that in the *Foreword* of the second edition of his already mentioned book, he sees it suitable to say:

> We believe we have managed to lay a firm foundation of the theory of this science, which is nothing but one of the two ways of looking at the world: the successive way beside the repetition way.[17]

The sequence is history (of humanity) and the permanence of the social world, the culture, the spirit and most important, of nature. The repetitive phenomena, coordinated by abstract laws, gradually become successive and permeate time – history. By classifying these phenomena using universal-individual coordinates, but also social-temporal, we can clearly see the transition between law and set: 1. Universal phenomena regarding space and time; 2. Universal phenomena regarding space, but individual regarding time; 3. Universal phenomena regarding space and individual regarding time; 4. Particular phenomena regarding both space and time. [18] But we are searching, not as much for the individual within history to relate to this universal, which belongs to science, but rather for the individual of the *experience* within history, which is historical and under a particular form, a general fact. In our opinion, if Xenopol's philosophy allows a counter-balance for the historical point of view that can reach Noica's second type of measure (the spirit's rebellion against human nature), we need to look for it precisely in the configuration of the term 'experience within history'. But, of course, the experience cannot be conceived without method. Experience, in general, is what widens the field of conscience, and the fact that even Kant considers it able to add something new to the concept and that it is the place where synthetic judges can be made[19] sheds even more light on the purpose of the criticism taken on by Xenopol. Maybe it is not as much a critique according to Kant, but rather an emphasis on the need for an inevitable critique of the historical act of knowing and a highlight of the method. However, widening the concept of experience and its synthetic value by recognising the synthetic purpose of the historical set represents a significant contribution. The two approaches we can use to take notice of the elements of experience within history are the reality of the historical field and the reality of science. The concepts used to describe repetition are partly valid for history as well (law,

---

[17] A.D. Xenopol, *Principiile fundamentale ale istoriei,* 2003, p. 37.
[18] Ibid., p. 46.
[19] C. Noica, *Schiță pentru istoria lui Cum e cu putință ceva nou* (A Sketch for the history of How is something new possible), (Bucharest: Humanitas, 1995), p. 227.

causality), but they acquire new traits when it comes to describing the historical way of being: causality (the relation forces-circumstances) is historical above all; natural law gets passed on as a principal through the set, and its epistemic swaying makes it suitable to describe not just history, but also the succession in nature. From now on, nature does not serve just as a mere support for experience, offering the process of making things general its primary resources to get to law; its phenomena and processes also have a successive side. Law's traits get taken over by the historical set, bound by the time factor. The realism Xenopol aims at is one of total experience, able to convert history into a whole science, one of the individual actions that obtain different levels of generalization through the set of development. By establishing history as an anti-theme to nature, Xenopol sets the premises of a philosophy that uses plenty of the second measure because it considers actions within history to be a measure of generalization and the set to have a universal meaning. If experience offers Hume (through habitude) the reasons to continue and unify conscience, retrieving the abstract representations in the individual of experience,[20] then the Romanian philosopher finds a generalization suitable to make science inside the action within history.

References

Noica, Constantin. 1991. *Pagini despre sufletul românesc* (Pages on the romanian soul). Bucharest: Humanitas Publishing House.

Noica, Constantin. 1992. *Mathesis sau bucuriile simple* (Mathesis or the simple joys). Bucharest: Humanitas Publishing House.

Noica, Constantin. 1995. *Schiță pentru istoria lui Cum e cu putință ceva nou* (A Sketch for the history of How is something new possible). Bucharest: Humanitas

Xenopol, Alexandru Dimitrie. 2003. *Principiile fundamentale ale istoriei* (The Fundamental Principles of History), translated into Romanian from French, introductive study and selected bibliography by Rodica Croitoru. Bucharest: Albatros.

---

[20] Ibid., p. 261.

CHAPTER V

TIME AND FREEDOM ACCORDING TO
C. RĂDULESCU-MOTRU AND M. HEIDEGGER

The discourse on time references the temporal reality in which history inserts the human way of being as self-becoming, along with a permanent effort to conceptualize the becoming itself within consciousness. The idea of history completes and provides multiple nuances to the general discourse based on temporality and culturally solicited by all the sciences. Philosophy, art and religion remain through the reference fields for expressing any significant text on temporality because time and space are connected categories, in the absence of which, we cannot have a systematic approach.

The reality understood as history matches the temporal reality; it is man confronting the becoming of his own being. However, referencing time, which 'captures' the human being inside its game, one much more suitable to self-relating – first of all to his freedom – is different from one century to another or from one cultural space to another.

Freedom and becoming

Freedom requires a temporal relation, as it can only be thought of in time. Becoming is a condition of the 'forthcoming', of bringing into the discussion (bringing into reality) the human possibility of existing in history, and a cultural necessity. The human being cannot get established in the absence of freedom. We can also reverse things and say that the concept of freedom would not have been possible without the man asking this fundamental question as the essence of his social being and the main condition (primordial) of self-expression. This question enables man to see the *truth* of his being and the value of truth as a possibility (or impossibility) to assert his self-awareness. To paraphrase Nietzsche, the issue of freedom is also axiological, not just epistemological – why do we want the truth and *not rather* the untruth (*Dincolo de bine şi de rău – Beyond good or bad)*; we can also state that non-freedom makes man extremely aware of stating his freedom in such a manner that it becomes faith. This need for affirmation can also be a 'prejudice' specific to metaphysicists: man's problems (and concepts) have a purpose, not for the transient historical circumstance but one *specific* to them – inside the Being. Just like it does in science (and history is a 'science' *also* reporting of freedom), liberty becomes faith; 'starting from this "faith", metaphysicists tend towards "science", that thing that will eventually be called "the Truth". [1]

Precisely where the human ideal of returning to self through culture (a system of values and of knowledge), one historically stated, intersects the history of this precise concept, there we find freedom, the principle of temporal (historical) 'non-transitivity': each period in time has its type of freedom. This concept obviously passes through any culture and remains a possibility opposing any constraint while gaining a transcendental characteristic. Therefore, man *is a possibility of freedom*, the right time (*Gelegenheit*) to transcend the historical time managed in the discourse and the time corrupted (persuaded to be a part of the individual expression) to express the being: 'Freedom is how *the Dasein* overcomes any particular existence and the entirety of being.' [2]

That can only mean that history cannot direct human beings towards a particular type of freedom, no matter how many culturally-objectified reasons it uses. However, from Heidegger's perspective, history – the history of the being or the history of metaphysics – is established as *Da-sein* (the being understood as an illuminating opening) and freedom.[3] The human being can still integrate time, which becomes vocation and destiny. In the modern era, after passing through the period deeply influenced by Cartesian determinism (very mechanistic) along with Christianity, destiny recovers the ancient elements but loses the reference model conceived then and especially its manner of ending. In those works of C. Rădulescu-Motru that directly ponder on destiny, the concept becomes a reference notion for the personalist vocation.[4]

---

[1] Vasile Tonoiu, *Înțelepciune versus filosofie* (Wisdom versus philosophy), (Bucharest: Publishing House of the Romanian Academy, 2007), p. 279.

[2] Michel Haar, *Heidegger și esența omului* (Heidegger and the essence of man), translated from French into Romanian by Laura Pamfil (Bucharest: Humanitas Publishing, 2003), p. 201.

[3] Ibid., p. 201–202.

[4] Constantin Rădulescu-Motru, *Timp și destin* (Time and Destiny), (Bucharest: Publishing House of the Foundation for Literature and Art 'Regele Carol al II-lea, 1940).

Destiny as the purpose of history

Time and destiny form a binomial equation that logically, historically, but mostly psychologically transcribes temporal reality. First, it is a time of nature, with its periodicity causally described and the legitimacy of its phenomena offering the possibility, to a particular limit, to mathematically represent them. Secondly, it is the time of historical becoming, that of the human desires, the 'the order of the spirit's unity'. Time is a convention, an agreement; it is the science of chronometry and consensus reduced to a number – therefore, it can get represented in space and becomes the fourth dimension of the space-time continuum. 'The temporal reality understood as destiny is the "life" of the soul's unity, the purpose of existence and the path to enrolling it within the order of finality.' [5]

From the perspective of temporal reality, finality has different meanings as long as we apply the limits of natural phenomena's laws. The predictability of natural sciences is based on this finality, and it also creates the paradigm of time from modern physics (the classical, Newtonian one). The homogeneous, abstract, Aristotelian time, passing with the objects of reality, the continuous and discontinuous time is still exterior and indifferent, equal and passive because it remains open to any interpretation.

> From the seeming evidence, time remains an enigmatic place of philosophy. However, the discourses on time tend to become rigid very fast. The so-called "issue of time" has been distributed on different levels and areas – physical time, experienced time, the time of the living beings and the being as being, the non-time time of the divine (eternity)… - that do not communicate much between themselves.[6]

Could there be a rift opening between the 'reflected on' time (the discourse on time) and the experienced time? *Quid est ergo tempus? Si nemo ex me querat, scio; si quaerenti explicare velim, nescio.*[7]

---

[5] On the other hand, according to Motru, time references the person and its purpose in culture and history: Viorel Cernica, *C. Rădulescu-Motru şi proiectul antropologic kantian* (C. Rădulescu-Motru and the Kantian anthropologic project), (Bucharest: Editor Mihai Dascăl, 2000), p. 107.

[6] Vasile Tonoiu, *Înţelepciune versus filosofie*, 2007, p. 281.

[7] Sfântul Augustin, *Confesiuni (Confessions)*, Book XI, Chapter XIV. See also Saint Augustine, *Confessions*, translated by Vernon J. Bourke, in „The Fathers of the Church", A New Translation, founded by Ludwig Schopp (Washington D.C.: The Catholic Univesity of America Press, 1953), p. 343 („What, then, is time? If no one asks me, I know; but, if want to explain it to a questioner, I do not know").

Seen as natural becoming, time (the relation time-movement) represents a set of trammels – as a result of its rigid determination – a way to explain the 'living' from the uninhabited object within the duration of the being (reasoning). The historical time, interpreted by Motru as destiny time, does not identify measured intervals extracted from the movement outlined by the image of science as accounts of equivalence and spatial-temporal balance.

> In the case of causal law, anticipation expects an equivalence rapport between cause and effect. In the case of destiny, this rapport is of different sorts because it does not weigh the number of material actions but the spiritual values that give purpose to the existence of man in the world. *Destiny does not ponder but justifies or condemns* (sub. n.).[8]

We have pointed out this nuance in Rădulescu-Motru's text only to relate it with the abovementioned idea, taken from Heidegger, of freedom understood as something possible or *Dasein*. Within this relation of 'semi-belonging' between man and being – 'the being makes thinking possible'[9] – the human essence does not get fulfilled, except through reasoning, and this has, here, a unique meaning of something that authorises and kind of condemns the man:

> The fact that the relationship with the being is immanent to the relationship that comes from the being results in the radical submission of reasoning – to which the second relation has been reduced – before the power of the being. The man is only able to think because the being makes him suitable to do so.[10]

Dasein – gateway to history

From the perspective of death, freedom precedes and anticipates any meaningful sentence. In reality, this is a double tautology: the first is metaphysical because we all know death accelerates any experience that includes a historical drama and overcomes it with a residue. That is precisely

---

[8] Constantin Rădulescu-Motru, *Opere alese* (Selected Works) (Scrieri filosofice românești, II – Romanian Philosophical Works), *Timp și destin* (Time and Destiny), edition supervised by Gh. Vlăduțescu, Alexandru Boboc, Sabin Totu (Bucharest: Publishing of the Romanian Academy, 2006), p. 118.

[9] Martin Heidegger, *Lettre sur l'humanisme* (Letter on Humanism), in „Questions" III, Paris, Gallimard Publishing, 1966, p. 79.

[10] Michel Haar, *Heidegger și esența omului*, 2003, p. 184.

why it conquers it for itself (for the man and the freedom of the being's reasoning).

> The everydayness of Dasein gets defined by absorption in Everyone. In the public arena of being-with-one-another, death is an established everyday encounter. This encounter gets interpreted as "one also dies someday". This "Everyone dies" harbours an ambiguity in itself, for this Everyone is just what never dies and never can die. Dasein says "Everyone dies" because this means "No one dies"; namely, not I myself. Death is something in being-with-one-another for which Everyone has already prepared a suitable interpretation.· In "Everyone dies", death is brought from the start to a level with the possibility of being, which in a sense, is no one's possibility. Death, concerning what it truly is, is thus driven away right from the start. "Everyone dies" is the interpretation in which Dasein re-Iabels its own most possibility for the public way of having things interpreted for everyday circulation, thereby driving its own most possibility away from itself. [11]

Because it happened *during his time,* the man got to be prepared for the *Dasein* cycle. Anything he thought of meant to liberate the being (the source of his freedom), but the circle ends right where it began: death decides the direction of each gesture before this could get fulfilled *in* time. The human being is a possibility of freedom and an occasion without which the being would remain in the shadows; 'more primordial in its essence than man', freedom becomes 'the possibility of a metaphysical truth'.[12] The time (history) of every action is not confined within the *Dasein* circle because it does not limit it but offers continuity through self-accomplishment and by 'settling' in the historical time. The freedom surrenders while at the same time giving it back to its initial way of being. However, the human being is not the one making the decisions, but rather the mean to reveal the truth of the being or the metaphysical truth. Freedom becomes a concept that goes beyond its traditional theories (free will, the absence of constraint, agreement with a metaphysical necessity etc.).

> The two concepts – *Da-sein*, generally understood as an illuminating gateway for the being and as freedom – are identified and comprehended as the foundation of History, the opposite concept of "nature". [13]

'Propelling' man in time and permeating history assumes the original freedom every time it happens, while man can remain faithful only to

---

[11] Martin Heidegger, *History of the Concept of Time. Prolegomena*, translated by Theodore Kisiel (Bloomington: Indiana University Press, 1985), p. 315.
[12] Michel Haar, *Heidegger şi esenţa omului*, 2003, p. 200.
[13] Ibid., p. 202.

himself as a ground-anchored being – the history of the Being (which contains the truth of man metaphysically expressed) takes over the human requests (thinking and taking action) thanks to its freedom of expression and becomes 'the history of the essential possibilities of a historical humanity'.[14]

However, is there a reversibility of Heidegger's time that turns to the 'peculiarity' of being 'freely constrained' (paradoxical association acquired after fulfilling a transcendental purpose by the historical man, 'settled' within the freedom of the being like he is always 'on his way towards something')?

> In choosing myself as my possibility, I choose my being. The possibility I choose as I run towards death is both confident and indefinite. To truly choose for me, I must align with the characteristics of that possibility in a genuine way, which means that the indefiniteness of death gets seized when I have understood the possibility as a possibility for every moment or when I am absolutely resolute in having chosen self. [15]

In other words, is there a negative time able to renew the truth of the purposeful historically revealed being (fulfilled in death) using the reverse side of acknowledging freedom?

This discussion on time concerning reality started from the analysis of C. Rădulescu, which allowed us to see destiny as a historical space-time continuum within the perimeter of culture and history. The experienced historical time, understood as destiny, becomes irreversible due to reasoning, which is *carried out* in history, and gives it a finality within the boundaries of freedom assumed by each individual. 'Individuality and the purpose of human life are based on experiencing time.'[16] In contrast to the time of nature and related to it, the time of human life does not represent some 'quanta' historically handled into a wave of becoming but signifies the originality of *this* experience and the precise time of each man. The structure of time as destiny nullifies the natural causality because it makes sense. That is more than a psychic causality; if it passes into the area of experienced reality (authentic), it results in manifesting the creativity's spontaneity of rhythm. W. Wundt, followed by Rădulescu-Motru up to a certain point, remains stuck in the correspondence nature-culture.

> To strengthen this correspondence, Wundt sees himself forced to oppose the constant unit of energy from the material world to a continuous increase of energy from the spiritual inner world, thus getting an equivalence between

---

[14] Ibid.
[15] M. Heidegger, *History of the Concept of Time. Prolegomena*, 1985, p. 318–319.
[16] C. Rădulescu-Motru, *Timp şi destin*, 2006, p. 183.

cause and effect on one side and a continuous increase through creative syntheses on the other.[17]

Nonetheless, when discussing destiny, Motru insists on not differentiating between the two forms right from the beginning because it would have led to an antithesis: abstract time and experienced time, or destiny. According to him, this distinction is not logically allowed as it creates confusion in understanding causality. The abstract physical time measured with instruments of modern sciences and thought about regarding movement is still aware of a certain periodicity and introduces the notions of uniformity and repetition. Motru's system, however, places it above time and perceives it as destiny. The latter is particular to perceiving uniqueness, but also a reality in its dimension, exceeding the factual, the mechanical periodicity, the assigning within a series and the addition. Moreover, this relation between the facts of experienced life understood as destiny brings about a different shade in dealing with life itself, able to modify even the thinking process in its effort to reflect another dimension. This dimension is 'the becoming' and it promotes such a succession, portrayed even through a geological becoming. As nations (organisms prone to becoming, whose temporality stands for destiny) grow old and die, the earth does not, but it 'modifies the spatial structure of the particles it is made of.' [18] Noticing this difference enables us to reopen the discussion on certain paradigms of dealing with reality. The modern paradigm focuses on explaining reality based on a subordination relation. The chain of causes and effects, together with legitimacy, offers science the possibility to predict. In the case of natural phenomena, determinism has a universal trait. Time gets reabsorbed within the game of causal subordination. The possibility of prediction makes science confident. However, subordination, legitimacy and causality lead to a 'fragmentation' of reality; laws are constructs that isolate facts from conditions and hypothetically built abstractions based on a necessary relation. This relation gets verified through experiment but is removed from the context and lacks complexity or contingent factors.

Many of these contingencies represent the substance, an environment that offers reality to the phenomenon. Time is how we intuit connections between actions and successive 'moments' as cause and effect; time is the mathematical one, the equation-time, physical, but not the substantial one, the result or the performance of the whole.

There were no stipulations in ancient times (Greek philosophy) nor legitimacy because 'the true precognition was based on the substance of

---

[17] Ibid., p. 182.

[18] C. Rădulescu-Motru, *Timp și destin*, 2006, p. 113.

things and knowing this through deduction you could explain any change in nature',[19] to quote Rădulescu-Motru. The quintessence of destiny was precisely this 'materialization' of the passing of time, non-other than duration, which again, fractures reality into segments and loses the intuition of the whole. Only this intuition is in itself living. Following this perspective, we can say that time is not 'wandering away' from a path where the flux of living always gets cast away, nor is it an analogy mathematically saved or a definition, but growth and meaning. Due to this growth, time comes back into its natural womb perceived as destiny because the 'materialistic' approach brings towards unity all of its energies (the natural valences, integrated into the individual) and outlines the field of authentic freedom. Liberty exists within destiny – even though, otherwise, we should consider it *a damnation of the way to be,* or destiny. However, it is not a damnation of the individual, torn between blind necessity and the voice coming from the Absolute (maybe of a god), nor is it a path forged between nature and the divine, but rather a possibility given by culture to add and assume (free) the spirit as a free cultivated direction – becoming and creation of its becoming.

The difference between time and destiny brings back into discussion another approach to becoming where the relation between the moments (diachronic landmarks) is not the same as that within the traditionally conceived causality. It is not a natural relation of subordination between cause and effect, but an integration, and internalisation that follows the pulse of the becoming and a tensioned tendency, an adjustment of the interior nature of purpose, as well as the *predisposition* of the means established to maintain the rhythm.

An issue arises: does time chooses its individuals and distribute them according to their aptitudes and predispositions to fulfil their destiny, or is it *becoming* at the same time as the individual? In other words, does time dispose of the individual, or does the individual dictate the rhythm? With respect to the causality relation that has undergone the forms of life and has permeated the bilogical level and the inside of the psychic tensions, the substance agrees with the conditions.

> The substance of life consists then in what has persistently sustained life for thousands of years on the surface of the earth, the typical conditions that have maintained the shape and the functions of the varied organisms. These shapes and functions do not get maintained on lived details but only on the persistence of the succession order. [20]

---

[19] Ibid., p. 114.
[20] Ibid., p. 121.

To which extent can we discuss the tyranny of time? There is no doubt it is a way for the becoming to become and for the fire to burn, but suspending this means rendering the combustion null. So, does form exist simultaneously with life, or does it transcend it? Time is not just a possibility. We can verify this within the creation. The predisposition and all the elements (let us call them talent or the capacity to create) can exist inside the individual and never manifest because they do not have their own time. Moreover, the destiny of a nation does not justify that nation in history because it is not yet in its history. Even though history does not wait, and it is not a gift you can just pick on your way, it is still the gift of time. The same tendency towards time and rhythm confirmation applies to the relation of destiny with life, destiny being out of tune. Life coincides with the desire to be free; it is the path taken by those who have reached (if they had a purpose of going somewhere) a point where they have to decide their faith (destiny); it is time on the verge of creation; it is the idea that sustains any history and that tendency towards a prophecy that gathers energies and forges vocations. Everything becomes simultaneously with itself, and it can be frustrating not to be there when time asks for it. 'There' (replaceable by then, then and there) is the beginning paradoxically, and only the beginning. It is that 'Adam-ism' that Cioran was talking about.

> Anything requires a beginning [...] Adam-ism can paralyze only the weak souls who lack visionary impulse, combative impulse and the will to get personal affirmation. It is not like it cannot induce crises or raise doubts, but it is revolting to remain without a word in front of it. [21]

Time is a possibility because, in its essence, it belongs to a whole. It exists inside the human being that maintains its path because it cannot get out, but particularly because it cannot stop. Although the ancient Greeks referred to time as destiny, it is important to note that time itself is not synonymous with fate or inevitability. Here is where the opposition of causalities also lays, between the two relative standards of time and becoming, in history and nature, between *sein-sollen*, that which 'must be' – history and moral life – and *sein*, in terms of nature. [22]

We will use the same type of approach to time to discuss the possibility of changing focus on the second part of the Cartesian expression *cogito sum,* even though this perspective could be dangerous, according to Heidegger.

---

[21] Emil Cioran, *Schimbarea la față a României* (The Transfiguration of Romania), (Bucharest: Humanitas Publishing, 1990), p. 40–41.
[22] See C. Rădulescu-Motru, *Timp și destin*, 2006, p. 119.

Motru believes that if we consider the possibilities of spiritual life (this *sein-sollen)* and attempt to make predictions concerning the becoming of the historical and moral life, then we must also consider the difference between the two types of sequence: that of the natural causality, described in quantity terms after an equivalence rapport between cause and effect and then the relation between the values, which implies another sequence, this time spiritual, that results in the *meaning* of life of the historical communities. Looking at things in terms of persistence – a substantial perspective – we need to exclude spaciousness and continuous repeatability that generate the universal law and stick to a *continuity* given by heredity, values and pursuits. These factors offer true durability and are initiated and achieved by the individual, but they do not necessarily end with *the same* individual. Natural causality has an objective, necessary and universal feature. Destiny is subjective, transcending the individual, but it starts from and returns to him. It is also unique and unitary.

> The most widespread catchphrase nowadays is: be through yourself what
> you have to be. That means that one should accomplish the substantial within
> himself. [23]

There is also a certain circularity within becoming that has to do, again, with a substantialist perspective and Motru notices it. It is not about the genetic structure, but more about the genesis of the cultural values. The spirit keeps its values – this is due to *the persistence* of conditions, the *sein-sollen*, and it gives them an archetypal trait. In nature, the theory retains the universalities, but in the spirit, 'the archetypes' passing through cultures impose an almost geometrical order, which according to Noica, it cannot be reduced to the natural order[24]. The possibility of finding similarities in

---

[23] Ibid., p. 117.

[24] 'The unificating', which is an archetype and it becomes the ideal of European culture (starting with Plato and continuing with Descartes and Leibniz until Husserls) is the 'nostalgia of one' belonging to Greek philosophy and conclusive for European culture because 'science belongs *to man*, culture is also his, as well as the laws of the Universe and its geometries'. We cannot say about the two types of culture – the historical opposed to the geometrical one – that they are irreconcilable, at least from the perspective of culture as history and the becoming towards spirit because, through history, the becoming (reasoning, the being) returns to itself and becomes becoming within the subject. This is where we look for the immanence, the last place and meaning of becoming and culture, the desire for order. 'Nature is not order and the astronomical worlds are not great mathematical congruencies, but the spirit is order and it gives rhythm to all realities that it takes into consideration.' How close is this approach to the substantialist idea, of asserting possibilities from and

historical descriptions (Thucydides, Tacitus), 'descriptions and portrayals of nations that we consider unaltered even today' is given by the persistence of spiritual 'substance' inside of which destiny is built. [25]

Why do we insist on this distance reality puts between itself and the attempts to offer itself, through a subject, a consolation for the inconsistency of any question that insists to separate it through time from time itself, just like a metaphysics of the eternal return, when time is not here, with it, nor is it close to any change? We must go back to what Cantemir was saying: time belongs to any change, but the eternal time (metaphysical) exists 'before any change can take place inside of it, because how else would one know that something is changing without knowing what time is?' [26] Time is not the receptacle of change, nor does it pass (run) along with reality, but exists within reality. Time understood as destiny is reality itself. In this way, as it grows and gives reality meaning, time becomes freedom and is accountable for accomplishing the desires of the whole from within. Destiny is unique and so is freedom, which cannot be equal to any time, nor separated from the times individually integrated; it cannot be on top, it cannot be something general, or it is general because it belongs to the individual as a whole. Therefore freedom is not a 'damnation' of the historical man, but it represents this possibility of man to manifest through the time that he has, the one his own being possesses. With respect to the *being*, something 'more primal than man', freedom does belong to the human and exists inside its being because this is the only way in which 'the *Da-sein* can surpass any particular living and also the totality of existences.' [27]

History becomes more than just a pretext for the subject, turned into its being. It is an aspiration that starts from within, not continuous decay and rush for the future or a broken piece from an atemporal fund from where the human being is trying to escape. [28] Essentially, this is a recurrent question

---

through the subject, is something that we need to ponder using the arguments of the circularity of the being and of the becoming within being, which brings reality into thinking and introduces the importance of 'done did' over the given and that of the subject. This direction can 'be followed throughout the entire plan of culture in extend', yet it is more clear in philosophy. See Constantin Noica, *Mathesis sau bucuriile simple* (Mathesis or the Simple Joys), (Bucharest: The Foundation for Art and Literature 'Regele Carol al II-lea', 1934), p. 9–16.

[25] C. Rădulescu-Motru, *Timp şi destin*, 2006, p. 118.

[26] Ibid., p. 149.

[27] M. Haar, *Heidegger şi esenţa omului*, 2003, pp. 200–201.

[28] See Marius Dobre, *Ideea de istorie la Emil Cioran* (The Idea of History according to Emil Cioran), 'Revista de filosofie' (The Philosophy Magazine), tom. LIV, nr. 1–2, 2007, pp. 104–105.

that goes beyond a purely deterministic reference because, being associated with the relativity of man's settlement into the becoming of nature (along the weak time, devouring its 'opponents'), it can only state one meaning, of the loss in time, and due to this, of any possibility, including history. This meaning cannot acquire epistemological values. The need to anticipate, to organize through the law, to arrange chaos through the reason constraining it to be determined and reasonable (a second tautology, of a liberty that proposes a purpose through man, but for a metaphysical 'man', that we believe it was brought forward by one statement made by Heidegger[29]), this is a necessity that ends up being a universal tyranny. Inside the universal we carry within (like we do in history), this tyranny becomes a 'loss' of the primordial time. If we accept the opinion of Motru and see time as destiny, we notice that time avoids bad relativity because it offers subject and history the possibility to *state* their own time. Out of a dumb interpretation of time (of its precarious relativity), we get many more other false interpretations, including time as a way to reference destiny and the possibility to know history.

> Each person has the tendency to understand time experienced in his/her own organic unity as the time of his/her spiritual life everywhere, so, without even knowing, the particular destiny of this "each person" elevates to the level of the destiny of the entire world.[30]

How can this relativity oppose history to man and contradict his actions, not just by his time, but also by the objective of science, perverting and making truth relative? It is not something new. The historical subject has always been frustrated with the historical pursuit, and even more with the political subject. Therefore, we end up stealing from history and the truth stating it, precisely the essence liberty is derived from, only to be able to understand the action and the deed. Just like Motru said, we might not end up like the Persian king Xerxes, who made his army beat the sea with rods 'because its waves impeded his fleet to go towards Greece',[31] nor like other ancient or even recent leaders who initiated prevention wars 'to act on a plan for their grandiose destiny', but we are at risk of understanding individual time as above the historical one, thus making history just an unnatural 'consequence' of our deeds (more or less deliberate, but well-founded by an ideology).

---

[29] See above, footnote 11.
[30] C. Rădulescu-Motru, *Timp și destin*, 2006, p. 209.
[31] Ibid., p. 210.

The best perspective on the time-freedom relation we can have is only possible within the history that brings this relation closer without forging it. Truth, historical fact and freedom, all have a purpose if we understand them correctly: they stand together to assert the subject as a creative entity, promoting values and truths that belong to it. Freedom does not mean justifying yourself at any cost, but the price one pays for self-knowledge, and the best we can get is the time able to include any historical action and the subject of this action at the same time.

References

Cernica, Viorel. 2000. *C. Rădulescu-Motru şi proiectul antropologic kantian* (C. Rădulescu-Motru and the Kantian anthropologic project). Bucharest: Editor Mihai Dascăl.

Cioran, Emil. 1990. *Schimbarea la faţă a României* (The Transfiguration of Romania). Bucharest: Humanitas Publishing.

Dobre, Marius. 2007. *Ideea de istorie la Emil Cioran* (The Idea of History according to Emil Cioran), 'Revista de filosofie' (The Philosophy Magazine), tom. LIV, nr. 1–2, 2007, pp. 104–105.

Haar, Michel. 2003. *Heidegger şi esenţa omului* (Heidegger and the essence of man), translated from French into Romanian by Laura Pamfil. Bucharest: Humanitas Publishing.

Heidegger, Martin. 1966. *Lettre sur l'humanisme* (Letter on Humanism), in „Questions" III. Paris: Gallimard Publishing.

Heidegger, Martin. 1985. *History of the Concept of Time. Prolegomena*, translated by Theodore Kisiel. Bloomington: Indiana University Press.

Noica, Constantin. 1934. *Mathesis sau bucuriile simple* (Mathesis or the Simple Joys). Bucharest: The Foundation for Art and Literature 'Regele Carol al II-lea'.

Rădulescu-Motru, Constantin. 1940. *Timp şi destin* (Time and Destiny). Bucharest: Publishing House of the Foundation for Literature and Art 'Regele Carol al II-lea.

Rădulescu-Motru, Constantin. 2006. *Opere alese* (Selected Works) (Scrieri filosofice româneşti, II – Romanian Philosophical Works), *Timp şi destin* (Time and Destiny), edition supervised by Gh. Vlăduţescu, Alexandru Boboc, Sabin Totu. Bucharest: Publishing of the Romanian Academy.

Saint Augustine. 1953. *Confessions,* translated by Vernon J. Bourke, in „The Fathers of The Church", A New Translation, founded by Ludwig Schopp. Washington D.C.: The Catholic Univesity of America Press.

Tonoiu, Vasile. 2007. *Înțelepciune versus filosofie* (Wisdom versus philosophy). Bucharest: Publishing House of the Romanian Academy.

CHAPTER VI

THE NOTION OF TIME ACCORDING TO RĂDULESCU-MOTRU AND BERGSON

To answer a fundamental question in the history of culture – What is time? – one could begin with ancient Greek philosophy or even earlier, with the mythological traditions that have been passed down through various nations. But since the issue of time is contemporary with the human's first inquiring startle and his first impulse in his confrontation with himself and the world was to determine the boundaries of his being and those of the human being in general inside space and time, then any question the human might ask himself has a direct or an indirect connection with a question about time. We are limiting our journey within history we set out for in the title to define time, up until Kant, heavily influenced by Greek philosophy, Plato and Aristotle especially. The latter considers time from a metaphysical perspective, while Plato sees time as the destiny of the 'polis' (the human), the substance's species, and the becoming as becoming. Kant underlines the boundary from our modern side on time through his criticism and the *a priori* categories, inherent to sensibility and intellect.

After Kant, modern culture, especially since Hegel, creates a radical antinomy with the whole previous period regarding the way it raises the issue of time. A more modern (and contemporary) way of conceiving time is that the concept is understood through a more significant rapport with the man (a psychological aspect) and then with the becoming within history. During this time, especially in the 19th century, the humanities, like the sciences of the spirit, the socio-human sciences, history etc. are searching for a methodology and a set of principles to base their knowledge on.

Noica understood the becoming within history (the becoming of man) as a power source for modern thinking, the cradle of philosophy.

Now, after Kant and through him, philosophy recaptured – differently than the Greeks – a particular state of its purity, comparable to a certain point to the Greek one. This time, the human being was not at play, but *the spirit* and the becoming of the spirit ended up being, in Hegel, that of the spirit revealed through history. Started by science, modern philosophy will end up in the becoming within history.[1]

We can qualify these two periods of time as cultural topoi when time has been firstly considered as time in time (the metaphysical aspect) and then as a time of man and history (the critical aspect).The two thinkers discussed here, Rădulescu-Motru and Bergson, develop a modern and contemporary side of the problem and relate, directly or indirectly, to a Kantian perspective, or rather post-Kantian, from the human's perspective and that of history, outlining a phenomenology significantly impacted on by the subject and its possibility to get set up in time.

That does not mean that modern thinking was not still metaphysically tempted to link time to the absolute, but paradoxically, the notions of destiny and continuance are of Greek origin. Motru, for example, places destiny inside a lexical family that describes becoming as an interior possibility[2] (a possibility of substance, sough-after by Aristotelian philosophy), starting, just like Bergson, a new categorization of the outlook on temporality, opposed to the previous one (physicalist at its core) where time had become a mathematical abstraction of movement in space.[3]

This modern approach to time, mixed with theoretical features that have meanings which carry the notion deep into the history of culture, gives Bergson's intuitionism and Motru's energetic personalism unforeseen tools for interpretation. As we move forward, we will only describe their general traits.

The Greeks viewed time from the perspective of substantialism, discussed only in relation to substance, as a category that could be impregnated by its quality. The substance is eternal; it is the principle that adheres to the being (after the Parmenidean definition); since time has to do with change, its being references otherness, becoming. In the Parmenidean category of human being, time is suspended as a principle, acquiring the traits of the being only through Plato's theories of participation and reminiscence – 'Parmenides has finally been left behind. The Doctrine of Ideas can unchain us from the Greek danger and spell, allowing the Ideas to

---

[1] Constantin Noica, *Trei introduceri la devenirea întru ființă* (Three Introductions to becoming within being), (Bucharest: Univers Publishing, 1984), p. 58.
[2] Constantin Rădulescu-Motru, *Timp și destin* (Time and destiny), in *Opere alese* (Selected Works), vol. II (Bucharest: Romanian Academy Publishing House, 2006), pp. 170–171.
[3] Henri Bergson, *Time and Free Will. An Essay on the Immediate Data of Consciousness,* translated by F.L. Pogson, M.A., (Dover Publications, Inc., 2001), pp. 100–104.

partake in one another, thus allowing life, synthesis and progress.' [4] The Parmenidean being is unique, immobile and eternal, and it excludes movement or becoming in a metaphysical way – eternity is the single mirror of the being. Similar to a monolith, the human being does not bring himself forward through objects and does not get conjugated alongside the other categories, including time, like in Aristotle. Heraclitus of Ephesus introduces a principled antagonism inside the human being. While Parmenides was formally trying to bring the human being into the light of the supreme certainty in opposition to the non-being, Heraclitus also uncovered its unseen face and entitled the non-being (contradiction, change, becoming) just as much as the being, to find a purpose in *logos*. For him, the fire, as name and principle, could always remain identical with itself (with the being). But fire also meant change, the being and the non-being were living under the same name (principle), which is both absolute and passing, eternal and flowing.

> In the sequence of his practice, Parmenides was just answering this question: how can the being be interpreted as being and existing and the non-being as non-being and non-existing? Therefore, the world (existence) was «covered», without it being part of the ontology field […]; and even if it was, it was not possible to notice it. [5]

Intuiting time is mandatory for Rădulescu-Motru in configuring the idea of destiny because, based on it, we can also represent to ourselves the difference between the two types of time: abstract, chronological and the experienced time, lived (psychological and historical), which is destiny. It is essential, according to him, for destiny to prevail in our representations right from the beginning because it actually is the initial form through which we have intuited becoming, the idea of real-time structured by a certain inherent periodicity of our inner life and later on through the constant repetitions in nature. Real and abstract time, derived from our first intuition previously imposed as destiny, is the result of our abstract thinking abilities; it is the time drained of all innermost determinations of life and living, and it is the astronomical, the mathematical, the time pertaining to mechanical causality. The two different ways of understanding time are nothing but the

---

[4] Constantin Noica, *Schiță pentru istoria lui Cum e cu putință ceva nou* (A Sketch for the history of How is something new possible), (Bucharest: Humanitas, 1995), pp. 81-82.

[5] Gh. Vlăduțescu, *Heraclit din Ephes, Cratylos din Athena, Antisthenes Heracliteanul. Mărturii și fragmente* (Heraclitus of Ephesus, Cratylos of Athens, Antisthenes the Heraclitean. Statetemnt and Fragments), (Bucharest: Romanian Academy Publishing House, 2008), p. 20.

result of a long cultural evolution, in Motru's opinion. It is also a distortion of our European culture that has seen in its science-established path a 'monarchic way' of a universal merge with reality; we might say that this way has deprived us of the deep intuition of our interior time. Nowadays, we can notice a certain epistemological superiority and self-sufficiency of the modern human, who looks down upon the old human living in his destiny, an attitude 'usually a grown man has towards a child. He looks down, almost with pity, upon what a few centuries ago was a serious preoccupation, even a torturous one for each soul.'[6] Even so, destiny comes back obsessively in the mind of the contemporary man. Just like the ancient human, the modern one cannot think of future changes in a chronological abstract way, nor can he scientifically divide his intimate life from those of others before him or those that will come after. This division has been fatal to us historically, but mostly culturally, as we gradually got used to intuiting time in its basic form, just like the Greeks had tried to impose. As opposed to time, destiny enforces an interior order; this got ingrained in the possibilities of our unique substance, which can also be the soul's substance. At some point, Motru says that the theory of destiny can be derived from the way Greeks (Aristotle) used to highlight the possibilities of substance when they had to explain becoming, just because they did not have the concept of developing law, nor that of modern scientific causality.[7] There is another order in nature. The difference between the two states can also be translated by what the Germans call *sein-sollen* – it must be and *sein* – what it is: is normally and necessarily natural in the matter, not in the life of the spirit.[8] Determining this difference is essential in thinking about destiny. That is why Motru has the option for a second notion, trying to bring it back to life, not necessarily through a hermeneutical effort (even though it exists in the first part of the book), but by building a concept. He considers destiny to prevail in man and in a nation, meaning in the human being in relation to becoming, which is subjectivity and achievement, thus being able to transcend the individual and even generations at a time. Similar to Bergson (on whose works Motru founded his discourse on time), the Romanian philosopher thinks intuiting time involves a deep interior breach, but for Motru, the duration (read as the duration of time as destiny) is important for becoming as a whole, for the individual's life *purpose* or for life seen as

---

[6] Nicolae Bagdasar, „*Timpul şi Destinul*" în viziunea lui C. Rădulescu-Motru („Time and destiny" in C. Rădulescu-Motru), Foreword for C. Rădulescu-Motru, *Timp şi destin* (Time and destiny), (Bucharest: Saeculum I. Q. and Vestala Publishing Houses, 1996), p. 18.

[7] C. Rădulescu-Motru, *Timp şi destin,* 2006, p. 114.

[8] Ibid., pp. 118–119.

history. Bergson sees duration as important only for our inner experience, as opposed to measured time.

Duration and destiny are contrary and complementary simultaneously, but their antinomy asserts itself. In our opinion, they complement each other because they are two concepts that indicate a new problem emerged from the modern take on time ever since Kant. This philosopher enriches the concept of time with a strong (fundamental) subjective assignation from a transcendental perspective, even though (like Bergson and Motru notice) the traits used to define time do not exclude it from the abstract frame of a scientific chronology and its temporality remains a subject, as a possibility in history or ability to create, as well as man's purpose and way of being in the world where he is becoming.

These two ways of understanding time – real-time and destiny-time – were never pondered upon simultaneously, so there is no theory to incorporate both. However, there is a connecting element in both: the relation time-movement.

The conscience of time is initially the conscience of destiny. Motru says it is positive that due to the first historians' approaches on the matter, along with those kept by mythological tradition, time complied with destiny in most European nations. That has not been studied enough by historians, philosophers, anthropologists or psychologists for that matter. Unlike the relativity that revolves around European modern culture (that also includes time in the system of the same relative and 'positive' values), prehistory and early history have drawn pretty visibly the frame inside which we can talk about time/destiny.

> The first rapports of time in these old traditions appear to be destiny. They represent the cosmogonic and ancient astrological beliefs, pretty well presented by historians. [9]

The Chaldeans, the Egyptians, the Etruscans, the Romans and even the Greeks had a substantialist early vision of time.

Time and Destiny

In order to make a comparison between the two approaches, one belonging to Bergson and the other to Rădulescu-Motru, we need to take notice of the emphasis they put on duration and destiny while trying to define the concepts. In emerging from the unique impulse of a mysterious past, duration always focuses on the beginning. The impulse amplifies with

---

[9] Ibid., p. 152.

every different nuance from anything that came before, just like a spring constantly designated by a distinct range (only that which continuously changes can last). With destiny though, all the tendencies focus on attaining the purpose. We can even state that duration highlights the beginning, when a moment rises to fill in another moment while destiny gathers as many tensions intensified by dispositions (elements of the individual or collective psyche, as well as spiritual values) focused on self-achievement or fulfilling a national condition.

Constantin Rădulescu-Motru's book, *Time and Destiny,* is the final part of his personalist-energy system that completes the other works meant to underline the distinction between 'the mechanical causality presumed by sciences (like physics and chemistry) and the psychic vital purpose.' [10] Other works that attain this kind of seamless insight are: *Puterea sufletească (The Power of the soul), Elemente de metafizică (Metaphysical elements), Personalismul energetic (Energist personalism),* and *Vocaţia, factor hotărâtor în cultura popoarelor* şi *Românismul (Vocation, a deciding factor for the culture of masses and the Romanian spirit).*

We can rephrase the primary argument of this book like this: time is measured differently in the life of individuals and communities, and it cannot be clarified in an abstract way, nor inserted into a numerical equation – sentence of the law in natural sciences – because time is part of an attempt to reach an individual or collective purpose, just like an assessment encoded inside the intimate substance we call interior life. Chronological notions cannot accurately translate the events of an individual's life.

> There is no sequence of historical actions like there is of psychical and chemical actions, which a science man can always identify as the same, but there is a life within history which along its course can become another one, just as the social group increases in number or gets older. [11]

The paper does not arouse speculative interest as much as it opens up new perspectives for sciences and disciplines on the verge of multiple subjects (psychology, sociology, history, anthropology), yet the fundamental questions get asked in philosophical terms. It represents more of an *aporia,* proposing several methodological solutions within the bounds of energistic personalism. Intuiting time is essential, but not like Bergson or Husserl; exploring phenomenology is done through experiments and proofs (arguments) that belong to experimental psychology or the history of philosophical concepts. The central point, the balance in the author's path

---

[10] Ibid., p.106.
[11] Ibid., p. 113.

is subjectivity aware of its own ethical and epistemic target, the representative for the man of vocation; in his previous book, *Vocation,* Motru presents vocational possibilities as social and cultural elements to define personality, while in *Time and Destiny,* we see ourselves inside a personalist ontology where man lives his own life according to his inner authentic rhythm accomplished as destiny. There is no hereditary vocation.

> A child comes into the world having individual aptitudes. Vocation results from combining his individual aptitudes towards a social purpose. In cases where society has not yet gained a unitary structure able to ignite a harmonious purpose in service of an ideal, there we cannot talk about vocations either. [12]

As elements of our inner life intertwine and our dispositions settle, time allows us to see the meaning of our inner evolution. But this is not the real-time, the chronology of biological actions which brings forth individual traits and potential, but another time, destiny.

Vocation and Becoming within History

Motru gives up his search for a method 'guide' based on the modern theories of time that could enable him to find conceptual parallelisms between abstract time and destiny. This last one cannot be reduced to a single statement that could capture the essence of temporality starting from natural causality. The requirements of these statements are linked to the idea that time is defined in a direct (or sometimes opposed) connection to space. This path in research was established by Aristotle, the same who also links time to the substantially pre-forming since any category (time pertains to being) and all things, in general, pertain to the supreme genus.

> And so if all thought is either practical or productive or theoretical, natural science would have to be some sort of theoretical science – but a theoretical science that is concerned with such being as is capable of being moved and with the substance that is in accord with its account holds for the most part only, because it is not separable. [13]

---

[12] Idem, *Vocaţia. Factor hotărâtor în cultura popoarelor* (Vocation, a deciding factor for the culture of masses and the Romanian spirit), in *Opere alese* (Selected Works), vol. II (Bucharest: Romanian Academy Publishing House, 2006), p. 73.
[13] Aristotle, *Metaphysics*, translated with Introduction and Notes by C.D.C. Reeve (Indianapolis/Cambridge: Hackett Publishing Company, Inc., 2016), p. 331.

Time is no exception. Destiny appears, thus, as pre-forming, setting itself in connection to potency, the way in which everything acquiring an ulterior determination gets confined to a substantially possible anteriority: the destiny (the time imprinted in our core substance) is the tendency to act upon the most intense and fundamental human aspirations. The possibility is a condition. No less accurate is to say that possibility may not happen (depending on the historical or the epistemic subject). Therefore, Motru believes that destiny, as it was previously dictated by the Greek Moirai, can also be fulfilled over generations, as well as not get fulfilled at all. Through his transcendental solution, even though he sets this capacity within the subject (using intuition, which chronologically organises reality), Kant is still unable to solve the issue of the rapport between becoming within self and the causality of science. According to Motru, this happens because, for Kant, time, as an *a priori* intuition, is assigned to transcendental consciousness, not proper to an individual one or a life experience determined within history. [14] Not even Bergson's intuition of duration can be a permanent solution for the Romanian philosopher. It does offer a starting point, susceptive to being enhanced by data from psychology, and it also becomes essential to a fundamental subfield, the psychology of creation. As a matter of fact, we can consistently detect the effects these psychological, sociological and anthropological data had on his work. Moreover, tackling the issue brings forward the main theories that have helped, throughout the history of philosophy to deepen and rethink the concept of time. All thesis and relative concepts of time are analysed, like the intuition of duration, perception and memory – they are all present in the reference works of that time: H. Bergson (*Essai sur les données immédiates de la conscience, Matière et mémoire*), Th. Ribot (*Les maladies de la mémoire*) or W. Wundt in whose experimental psychology laboratory worked Motru as well.

The array of distinct fields discussing time and the historical topos where time gets configured is way more diverse. The main idea that keeps reappearing, like a leitmotif, is how substantial are the structures of both time and the spirit (individual or of the people). Out of all these various traits of history and of our soul (will-powers collide, vocations, temperaments), we can see purpose standing out, a rhythm of becoming in which the individual/the nation consumes its being: he/it is destined to fulfil this order; inside of it, he slowly and definitely resorbs himself throughout his existence. The purpose of destiny in the life of an individual/community is to conduct and accomplish cognitive grounds and moral imperatives, but especially the

---

[14] C. Rădulescu-Motru, *Timp și destin*, 2006, p.129.

spiritual values; time-destiny cannot get separated from vocation. The formula for time and vocation – a matter of great importance in the field of energetic personalism – can be addressed using its approximate term: destiny. Only that in terms of modern philosophy, even though destiny takes on the entire spectrum of significances existing in the mythology of every nation (especially the Greek one), along with the elements of time understood as destiny by the substantial side of Greek philosophy, the concept of destiny is new, precisely thanks to the traits of the other notion, vocation. Understood within the boundaries of the Aristotelian concept of *entelechy* destiny still preserves two important meanings, present in the mind of the ancient Greek, as well as in later theories that have probed this reality: the course and the accomplishment of the individual life and life within history. They are both considered part of the spiritual values and of ethical imperatives.

For Aristotle, time is still part of the absolute genres, as a category but also a participant to being through the particular. For him, the Universal does not exist, except within the particular, unlike Plato, for whom the Universal can exist purely on its own. Thus, when talking about time, like we can talk about the other categories as well, time and space remain inside things. When discussing anteriority,[15] the first meaning (the proper bearing) is set after time, and the second is after the layout of the sequence. In this way, simultaneity imposes becoming at the same time upon the intellect as a proper bearing, just like, within the movement (time is the number of movements), the first out of the six modes is a generation.[16] Still, movement can only be considered according to quantity, quality and place, not concerning substance. The rapport of time and other categories, especially existence (the substance), has suffered different adjustments from Aristotle to Kant. The most eloquent approach though belongs to Kant (paradoxically, apriorism closely relates time to a permanence that has to do with the transcendental substance). Bergson's duration takes yet another step towards making time substantial, going from the transcendental to the individual subject – experiencing time no longer belongs to consciousness in general, but becomes an individual experience and creation, unique and non-recurring. But intuiting time consists of just as many nuances (levels) that cover reality, offering its moments in the same order we use to define it. We do not describe it as a sequence or an order in sequence, nor as a number of the sequence, but as a structure (in consciousness) of some specific rapports, mainly and first of all cultural. 'Intuiting time is a build-up of rapports; a build-up which is the work of human activity in the cultural

---

[15] Aristotle, *Categories and Interpretatitione*, translated with Notes by J.L. Ackrill, Claredon Press. Oxford, Oxford University Press Inc., New York, 1963, p. 39.
[16] *Ibidem*, pp. 39-41.

field.' [17] If we go through all the stages in history when theories on time have emerged – considered until and after Kant to be movement rapports, real-time, abstract chronology – we can form a synthesis of the nature of abstract time (real or revolving, in Noica's terms) with Noica's help: it is not as much an ordinal number as it is an order; and not as much an order of sequence, but the sequence, and finally, connection in succession.[18]

What are the components that work together to realise the intuition of destiny? Motru says there are three ancient factors at the basis of destiny:

a) destiny contributes to asserting life, which thus acquires first-level value compared to the whole universe;
b) the individual/the group compliant with destiny gains consciousness of the fact that life is irreversible;
c) intuiting destiny is mystical.[19]

For the human that has just overcome the prehistoric era, predicting destiny is a way of building the reality inside the transient without reason-technical means, 'a mystical anticipation of the universal becoming'.[20]

Our inner life and universal order form an organic entity. From a substantialist point of view, this entity contains the elements that also define it as temporality; time-destiny means positive subjectivity, experiencing and predicting, which at the beginning had a powerful mystical trait. In considering destiny, the accent falls on the subjective. In the first stages, when man built his temporal reality, he allowed reason to distinguish a separate side of temporality, much more abstract, that opposes and separates from the subjective time-destiny, conceived as real objective time. Experiencing destiny gets left in the shadow, while abstract time replaces, at least in the sciences, the preoccupation with destiny.

Real, abstract, mathematical time, objective and equal to itself, is the time of mechanical determinism, causality and natural laws. The scientist prefers real, chronological time over destiny. But, after studying the variety of temporal nuances (also including, besides the physical time, the psychological, historical, physiological, biological, and that of civilisations or the time of culture), he can notice the mix between objective and subjective in conceiving all of these times, which might as well be the times of life – that contains in itself the notion of destiny – and shifts from the sciences of life towards the probabilistic physics of quantum phenomena.

---

[17] C. Rădulescu-Motru, *Timp și destin*, 2006, p. 154.
[18] Constantin Noica, *Trei introduceri la devenirea întru ființă*, 1984.
[19] C. Rădulescu-Motru, *Timp și destin,* 2006, pp. 173–174.
[20] Ibid., p. 169.

According to Motru, resorting to destiny is a necessity of contemporary science. It needs to be separated from mystical beliefs and evolve from "a simple disguise of merciless Moira", to a time of phenomena of the alive, of cultural and psychical life and becoming within history. Moreover, statements referencing destiny are easy to find all across history, up until the present day. The best place to find intuition within history is in monotheist religious beliefs, where divine power is a disguise of destiny.[21] The presence of destiny is also found in theories on the unconscious, but there is a difference: the ancient beliefs saw predestination as a sentence from divinity while the unconscious confronts man with the physiological underlayer of mental functions. However, the most visible appeal to the idea or the metaphor of destiny remains in the political and social ideologies of today. In this case, destiny is no longer a mystical proclamation, an oracle or a charm, but 'a slogan of the propaganda supporting some ideology'.[22]

We notice that while talking about destiny, we need to consider a potential existential tension, as well as an epistemological one, created by two notions: real chronological time and the time of social and cultural life. Not just Motru, but Bergson also notices this duality that takes over (implicitly or explicitly) the opposition gradually developed of other pair of contradictory notions, and all the contradictions finally come down to discussing the antinomy objective/subjective. On the objective side, we have truth, universal (general), reason, ideal, and substance. Real, abstract and objective time is the time of reason. The subjective, closely tied to duration and destiny, implies concepts like relative, individual, irrational and unconscious. However, paradoxically, after reading the works of both Motru and Bergson, we notice that duration and destiny, even though opposed to the real, abstract, spatial, chronological and mathematical time, they do not oppose substance. As both have their origins in the subject, destiny and duration are subjective, as much as they belong to the subject (just like all the other categories). But, for Aristotle, the subject is *inside* reality, not *opposed to* reality: it is 'the under layer (*hypokèimenon*), the substance, therefore reality in itself, and moreover, the object, strictly in its present-day meaning'.[23] We have already seen that destiny is substantial, even though it lies in the subject, precisely as subject is the support and the purpose of reality. The subject is not a phenomenon, but a substance. Experienced time, intuited as destiny or as duration, is the subjective time. Actually, destiny and duration only make partial contact with each other as

---

[21] Ibid., p. 172.
[22] Mircea Florian, *Recesivitatea ca structură a lumii* (Recession as a structure of the world), vol. I (Bucharest, Foundation Pro Publishing, 2003), p. 219.
[23] Ibid., p. 173.

significance, but through continuous creation (Bergson) and the personification of energetic substance (Motru), they both define the same inner temporality. We cannot describe the inside of things in a Kantian way, using subjective time. However, if we consider it *apriori* (and no longer destiny and duration) as a time of transcendental consciousness, we can exhaust its determinations and thus transform it into a form of intuition. The time-destiny acknowledges the subject it proposes to the world and creates it permanently. The creations of the actual subject, experienced as destiny and expressed in duration, do not become objects in themselves but actions of the self or history. Transcendentally speaking, the synthesis applies to the subject and nothing but the subject; time belongs to sensibility, not the living. It can much less facilitate knowing the object in itself.

Duration – perpetual creation

Usually, philosophy books associate Henri Bergson (1859–1941) with intuitionism and the philosophy of life. His most important works suggest a metaphysics whose solutions go beyond traditional logic, at least within the limits of the theory of knowledge and recommend the overcoming of the intellect's logic.[24]

> Bergson's theory on the intellect is correct and even subtle. He is able to see the connection between the intellect and mathematics [...] and also the one between the intellect, the inorganic matter and mechanical movement.[25]

but his notion of intellect does not surpass intuition, because he thinks that universal logic should be overcome and replaced with a new 'science of the spirit', as suggested in his own words. Bergson's metaphysics prefers notions (concepts) designed particularly for a new philosophy of life, which should move past the rigid frame imposed by the intellectual evolution, that represents knowledge in space: a true evolution creates in other dimensions, through the intuition of pure duration.

---

[24] His most important works: *Eseu asupra datelor imediate ale conştiinţei* (Essay on the immidiate data of counsciousness), his first Phd in Letters, defended in 1889; *Materie şi memorie* (Matter and memory) (1896); *Râsul* (The Laughter) (1900); *Evoluţia creatoare* (The creating evolution) (1907); *Energia spirituală* (The spiritual energy) (1919); *Durată şi simultaneitate* (Duration and simultaneity) (1922); *Gândirea şi mişcarea* (Thought and movement), (1934).
[25] Alexandru Surdu, *Filosofia contemporană* (Contemporary Philosophy), edited and a foreword by Viorel Vizureanu (Bucharest: Paideia Publishing, 2003), p. 34.

The creationist moment of duration fulfils better within the frame of artistic activities. The artist can often intuit an authentic experience and express or suggest it with his artistic means, thus managing to cross the border the spirit has put between him and the pure duration. [...] We live as much as we are able to continuously create ourselves.[26]

Bergson's *duration* does not resume the old perceptions of time but demolishes them by discovering within time and movement the 'not allowed' spatial representation and exteriorisation of the pure duration. He says time was conceived as a fourth dimension of space, the intellect's logic (abstract, rigid, quantifiable and applicable to mathematics). This logic eliminates the experience (intuition) of our inner duration and confuses it with measure, leading sequence to be identified with spontaneity and quality with quantity. Thus, Bergson feels obligated to find a solution to justify experiencing pure duration, to resolve the schematic arrangement of abstract thinking and its logical, rigid patterns that represent space, and also to separate time from space (time is a measure of sequence ever since Aristotle: abstract mathematical time is the measure of movement). The sentence about experiencing duration is stated as a final solution because it is a natural consequence of all the other results of thought, amongst which the worst is time representing space (attaching duration to a number or quantity).

Abstract time is not a psychological time. The *a priori* intuition of time, Kant's solution, negates experience and decisively contributes to defining time, even though it can partially help us understand its nature. Time type of sensibility predates the inner and the outer experience. Time is not an empirical concept we can somehow draw from an experience. For simultaneity or succession would not themselves come into perception if the representation of time did not ground them a priori. Only under its presupposition can one represent that several things exist at the same time (simultaneously) or at different times (successively). Time is a necessary representation that grounds all intuitions. In regard to appearances in general, one cannot remove time, though one can very well take appearances away from time. Time is therefore given apriori. In it alone is all actuality of appearances possible. The latter could all disappear, but time itself, as the universal condition of their possibility, cannot be removed.[27]

---

[26] Ibid., p. 35.
[27] Immanuel Kant, *Critique of pure reason,* translated and edited by Paul Guyer, University of Pennsylvania, Allen W. Wood (Yale University: Cambridge University Press, 1998), p. 162.

The connection between destiny and creation is another aspect of duration that we need to examine. It is partially included in *L'évolution créatrice*. If we look beyond the apparent paradox, we might notice the natural intertwining of creation and destiny, provided that we remove the *preformationary* meaning from the concept of destiny and consider the *epigenetic* one: 'everybody's life has its rhythm, and this rhythm determines if the person will arrive later than another and occupy a certain place'.[28]

For Bergson, the inner dynamic, perceived as an intensive duration harmoniously integrated, excludes the idea of time as a linear passing from one moment to another like a mechanical and monotonous sequence, no matter from which perspective you are looking at it. The inner time is not a metronomic beat but development and merger under creation. The symphonic aspect of becoming – every moment is contained within the following, not adjacent to it – together with living under tension and intensity (like replaying the theme of a polyphonic piece) should be understood by the individual as themes of self-creation and as achievements that assume time as a conscious and exciting victory over each moment conquered. The tendency to mainly notice abstract congested fragments while dynamically perceiving our life comes from physics. Time is adjacent to space, but moments are mathematical sentences for feelings and states.

> For if time, as the reflective consciousness represents it, is a medium in which our conscious states form a discrete series so as to admit of being counted, and if on the other hand, our conception of number ends in spreading out in space everything which can get directly counted, it is to be presumed that time, understood in the sense of a medium in which we make distinctions and count, is nothing but space.[29]

Bergson sees Kant's apriorism as a construction where the value of consciousness as an experienced mental activity has no significance. Kant's temporal sequence is an abstract mechanic, related to the one describing special simultaneity. It is a juxtaposition of moments in space. The moments of awareness follow each other mathematically, which is irreversible (according to strict logic based on the building of conscience in general). The conscience actions and everything we experience are engaged in this, but they lack their dimension, able to provide identity and authenticity. Apriorism

---

[28] Mircea Florian, *Experiența ca principiu de reconstrucție filosofică* (Experience seen as principle for philosophycal reconstruction), (Bucharest: Gramar Publishing, 2002), pp. 283-284.

[29] Henri Bergson, *Time and Free Will. An Essay on the Immediate Data of Consciousness*, authorized translation by F.L. Pogson, M.A. (Dover Publication, Inc., Mineola, N.Y., 2001), p. 91.

denies individual consciousness of creative participation and implication in building inner experiences. Kant's time is an 'abstract mathematical time, used as a measuring tool by mechanical sciences, not the time found inside soul experiencing.'[30] Therefore, inner and outer experiences are both 'formatted' according to the principle of transcendental intuition. Since conscience, in general, references something abstract, inner freedom and creative force get left in the dark. Well, they do not actually exist; there is freedom and creation only within the limits of abstract morality, which is also separated from time and space since it is a world generated by the law of categorical necessity, with connections as flexible as the trajectory of stars in the sky described by Newton's mechanic. For Kant, experience is not an active part of building the concept of time. Bergson develops the concept of time as something growing from within, recreating itself with every experience, without becoming alienated by it. For him, time is quality in duration, related strictly to consciousness: none of its new parts is identical, nor immobile, but it integrates itself into an amplified harmony using the intuition that grows precisely out of the abundance of experiences gathered as a whole in their complexity and unable to happen again (non-recurring).[31] Therefore, Bergson's duration does not want to replace one notion with another. He does not want to replace the abstract, mathematical time associated with Newtonian mechanics with a psychological representation of time, but this representation is, in fact, *the duration,* constantly perceived differently but always growing and accumulating as a whole. What does the wholeness of this representation have to offer? Is not it just a piecing together of scattered elements after the demolition of transcendental aesthetics gathered into a new concept? Kant was also able to solve some contradictions in representing time. Some of these contradictions got the support of the empirics and their tendency to use experiments in science. Another way was the lack of conceptual means to capture the diversity of representing time (in psychology, physiology, economy, history etc.), together with the ability to bring time to the unity of conscience with its typical and cognitive functions. Bergson's intuition of duration was considered an unusual solution, unlike transcendental aesthetics and the a *priori* ways of representing time, seen as a step forward in solving this issue for which sciences, especially Kant's contemporary philosophy, had no solution:

> The real psychological time consists, according to Bergson, in sensing the duration of an experience. Sensing the duration [...] has no further

---

[30] Constantin Rădulescu-Motru, *Timp și destin*, 2006, p. 129.
[31] Pete A. Y. Gunter, *Bergson and Jung*, in *Journal of the History of Ideas*, vol. 43, nr. 4, Oct.–Dec., 1982, p. 635.

connection to the physical time than the one existing between an authentic action and its notion. A notion is abstract and thus able to help isolate and classify psychological time, but nothing more. It can never replace it.[32]

Bergson's option for defining duration lies in marking the boundaries between the consciousness abstractive power – extending reason into the universal represented on the level of the essence – and the capacity of intension represented (experienced) individually and still as a result (intention, direction, existential tension and cognitive adjusting) of a genetic accumulation: duration consists of the intensity of life that does not get consumed within the individual; duration is the accumulation of life through everybody's experiences, as a type. Duration is a tendency and perpetual change. Only what changes can last; the sequence is not an accumulation of causes and effects in time, as this sequence immobilizes time and does not give back its duration but only as an abstract measure of the outer accumulation. Therefore, we do not have a definition which restricts the concept to an abstract name, but an intuitive disclosure, similar to art, intuitive and creative at the same time, able to give us back the reality of duration.

The reference point in Bergson's concept of time is Kant's apriorism. The importance of distinguishing the ways to approach time articulated in *The Critique of the Power of Judgment* also has a scientific signification because it sets a historical ground for a new issue, this time belonging to humanistic studies. Kant's premise is not that of a time made more substantial, but of a time of relation: the traditional 'qualities' of time, as defined ever since Aristotle like non-reversible, unidimensional and successive adjacency are kept, but the accent falls on the subject, whose temporal projection puts order into perception: the synthesis gets done on the level of intuition, before experience. Bergson's quarrel with this is the formalism introduced by the subject: contrary to all expectations, time is not an objective 'distortion', but an arrangement rigorously proved, a rationalist developing of the principles of causality proper to Newtonian science. *The Essay on the Immediate Data of Consciousness*[33] suggests we should separate science from consciousness, duration from time defined by spacial patterns. Duration is always the same and yet different because it does not cover successive instant moments frozen like the beats of a metronome, but every one of its elements contains the whole; every one of its elements gathers change into an organic and coherent bunch. Otherwise, if analyzed too closely, the movement can become an aporia.

---

[32] C. Rădulescu-Motru, *Timp și destin*, 2006, p. 139.

[33] Henri Bergson, *Time and Free Will. An Essay on the Immediate Data of Consciousness*, 2001.

Why resort to a metaphysical hypothesis, however ingenious, about the nature of space, time, and motion, when immediate intuition shows us motion within duration and duration outside space? There is no need to assume a limit to the divisibility of concrete space; we can admit that it is infinitely divisible, provided that we make a distinction between the simultaneous positions of the two moving bodies, which are in fact in space, and their movements, which cannot occupy space, being duration rather than extent, quality and not quantity. To measure the velocity of a movement, as we shall see, is simply to ascertain a simultaneity; to introduce this velocity into calculations is simply to use a convenient means of anticipating a simultaneity.[34]

Change generates discomfort for the spirit. But change per se cannot be perceived, only its reflexes in things; the results of change seduce the spirit, but within these results, movement (change, becoming, creation in action) is frozen and fixed. The spirit can create within a duration. From *L'évolution créatrice* we find out that change is the pure duration and the opposition between time and duration, or space and time, that leads to the opposition between spirit and matter, can also be interpreted in terms of the late scholastic antinomy when the spirit is a pure duration (affirmation, creation), a permanent inner activity opposing the external negation and the continuous resistance to change represented by matter.[35]

Intuiting time implies order, structure and connections determined by a consciousness that cannot exist in the absence of a cultural field. However, it is not easy to define the ridge between sensing duration and the duration of cultural creation (the necessary time to elaborate and the duration of cultural feedback / determining the value). We cannot understand the structure of time unless we study *the times.* Therefore, there are multiple diverse and complex relations that together, help us understand time as it is. There have been several mentions of a biological time (tempo vital) which cannot get separated from the physical one, but the most complex is the psychological time.

In order to define the concept of time in relation to movement and to format the temporal sequence, we need to use the notion of causality. For Kant, this is a category of the intellect that makes experience possible. Within experience there is also time, a delicate reinforcement of the relation cause/effect, and this relation gets replaced by a logical one: if A, then B.

---

[34] Ibid., p. 114.
[35] A.W. Moore, *Bergson and Pragmatism*, in „The Philosophical Review", vol. 21, no. 4 (Jul. 1912), p. 399.

Using causality we cannot understand how the switch from A to B takes
place, but we get pressured by the nature of our thinking to establish that the
two form a necessary pair. [36]

The necessity of this connection is rational above all, although it starts
from an act of experience. Consciousness (reason) thinks that the link
between cause and effect is the general, which signifies a necessary
repetition or the ability to make it abstract through numbers.

As the successive phases of our conscious life, although interpenetrating,
correspond individually to an oscillation of the pendulum which occurs at
the same time, and as, moreover, these oscillations are sharply distinguished
from one another, we get into the habit of setting up the same distinction
between the successive moments of our conscious life: the oscillations of the
pendulum break it up, so to speak, into parts external to one another: hence the
mistaken idea of a homogeneous inner duration, similar to space, the moments
of which are identical and follow, without penetrating, one another.[37]

Bergson thinks the necessity created by consciousness between the
elements that oppose sequence is identical to that creating a unitary (opposed
to and beyond the diversity offered by experience, the way in which we
become aware of phenomena in sensations) environment for the coexisting
phenomena. But within this structural unity, space and time influence and
affect each other according to transcendental aesthetics.

'There is a real duration, the heterogeneous moments of which permeate one
another; each moment, however, can be brought into relation with a state of
the external world which is contemporary and can get separated from the
other moments in consequence of this very process. The comparison of these
two realities gives rise to a symbolic representation of duration, derived from
space. Duration thus assumes the illusory form of a homogeneous medium,
and the connecting link between these two terms, space and duration, is
simultaneity, which might get defined as the intersection of time and
space.'[38]

Mutual altering of both concepts is a crucial observation that has led to
quarrels over the course of the history of philosophy. Movement (a critical

---

[36] Claudiu Baciu, *Semnificaţii ale conceptului de libertate la Kan* (Signification of
the concept of freedom in Kant), in Studii de istorie a filosofiei universale (History
studies of universal philosophy), coord. Alexandru Boboc, Nicolae I. Mariş,
(Bucharest: The Romanian Academy Publishing, 2003), p. 68.
[37] H. Bergson, *Time and Free Will. An Essay on the Immediate Data of Consciousness*,
2001, p. 109.
[38] Ibid., p. 110.

ally of physical time, but not only) brings the same efficient support to both notions, space and time.

Einstein's formula, $e = mc^2$ is a wonderful illustration of this alliance that postulates the indestructible bond between space and movement as time coexists with space within this binomial, specifically by being its fourth dimension. However, Bergson tends to annihilate this physical and mathematical unity of the two concepts by stating that our inner reality, purely psychological, manifested through the sequence of moments, is not a linear change (adjoining) but a dynamical sequence. Perceived on the inside, this dynamic underlines the fluidity and fluency of experienced time. By being exterior and unitary, the flow of space-time (analysed through movement) generated the mechanical disintegration of the moment, just like the Greek aporiae. In Bergson's words, Zenon reconstitutes Achilles' moves from diverse, separated segments, leaving aside the basic, inseparable unity of each step the hero took, who, after a certain number of the same actions, can catch up with the turtle.[39] Bergson's duration is action in time, unable to algebraically recompose. The standard of adjoining moments can become illustrated by a musical production of the human souls, where each moment gets embedded in the next, and perceiving the whole (the symphony) – and understanding it – is a seamless act, able to see the structure within the becoming, not keen on taking it apart in order to analyse it. Therefore, this is how Bergson opens up like a window towards capturing (representing) an ontological and humane profoundness, which has yet to be explored, having time as a measure of inner mobility[40] inside which the ego disappears, covered by a thick shadow emerging from the unconscious.

References

Aristotle. 2016. *Metaphysics*, translated with Introduction and Notes by C.D.C. Reeve. Indianapolis/Cambridge: Hackett Publishing Company, Inc.

Aristotle. 1963. *Categories and Interpretatitione*, translated with Notes by J.L. Ackrill, Claredon Press. Oxford, Oxford University Press Inc., New York.

Baciu, Claudiu. 2003. *Semnificații ale conceptului de libertate la Kan* (Signification of the concept of freedom in Kant), in *Studii de istorie a filosofiei universale* (History studies of universal philosophy), coord.

---

[39] Ibid., pp. 113-115.
[40] Maurice Blanchot, Joel A. Hunt, *Bergson and Symbolism*, in *Yale French Studies*, no. 4, *Literature and Ideas*, 1949, p. 63.

Alexandru Boboc, Nicolae I. Mariş. Bucharest: The Romanian Academy Publishing.

Bagdasar, Nicolae. 1996. „*Timpul şi Destinul*" *în viziunea lui C. Rădulescu-Motru* („Time and destiny" in C. Rădulescu-Motru), Foreword for C. Rădulescu-Motru, *Timp şi destin* (Time and destiny. Bucharest: Saeculum I. Q. and Vestala Publishing Houses.

Bergson, Henri. 2001. *Time and Free Will. An Essay on the Immediate Data of Conssciouness,* translated by F.L. Pogson, M.A. Dover Publicatioons, Inc.

Blanchot, Maurice; Joel A. Hunt. 1949. *Bergson and Symbolism*, in *Yale French Studies*, no. 4, *Literature and Ideas*.

Florian, Mircea. 2002. *Experienţa ca principiu de reconstrucţie filosofică* (Experience seen as principle for philosophical reconstruction). Bucharest: Grammar Publishing. Pete A. Y. Gunter. 1982. *Bergson and Jung*, in *Journal of the History of Ideas*, vol. 43, nr. 4, Oct.–Dec.

Florian, Mircea. 2003. *Recesivitatea ca structură a lumii* (Recession as a structure of the world), vol. I. Bucharest: Foundation Pro Publishing.

Kant, Immanuel. 1998. *Critique of pure reason,* translated and edited by Paul Guyer, University of Pennsylvania, Allen W. Wood. Yale University: Cambridge University Press.

Moore, A.W. 1912. *Bergson and Pragmatism*, in "The Philosophical Review", vol. 21, no. 4 (Jul. 1912).

Noica, Constantin. 1984. *Trei introduceri la devenirea întru fiinţă* (Three Introductions to becoming within being). Bucharest: Univers Publishing.

Noica, Constantin. 1995. *Schiţă pentru istoria lui Cum e cu putinţă ceva nou* (A Sketch for the history of How is something new possible). Bucharest: Humanitas.

Rădulescu-Motru, Constantin. 2006. *Timp şi destin* (Time and destiny), in *Opere alese* (Selected Works), vol. II. Bucharest: Romanian Academy Publishing House.

Rădulescu-Motru, Constantin. 2006. *Vocaţia. Factor hotărâtor în cultura popoarelor* (Vocation, a deciding factor for the culture of masses and the Romanian spirit), in *Opere alese* (Selected Works), vol. II. Bucharest: Romanian Academy Publishing House.

Surdu, Alexandru. 2003. *Filosofia contemporană* (Contemporary Philosophy), edited and a foreword by Viorel Vizureanu. Bucharest: Paideia Publishing.

CHAPTER VII

TIME AND HISTORICAL EXPERIENCE

Instead of conclusion

A fundamental question, almost the same now as it was three thousand years ago, would be the following: does time juxtapose the moments of our existence to preserve the truth of our being in history? If it does, then to what extent does history contribute to the inner truth? And if the moments are juxtaposed, is there a link between them? Are we victims of becoming, or is there a link between self-becoming and Reason? The experience with time does not make us happier than we were at the dawn of history. On the contrary, one could say that we are now more puzzled that we gradually approach the end of history, which will devour us with all our truths, as Chronos, at the mythological beginning of civilization, devoured his offspring.

The present book suggests the idea of a history which revolts against time. The author searches for a meaning for the historical becoming and the self-becoming. In doing so, he does not claim his questions are original, provided that new ones are not necessarily essential. The core of our experience with time is a permanent dialogue with us and our fellow creatures. There is a circularity of the great truths of being, noticed by Noica. Though what Noica did was to confirm, in his way, a much older truth that could be found in Plato. This truth is related to the fact that, inside our being, time has its sense: it *becomes* logical time, in which the present disappears; only the past and the future are the legitimate topics of the logical time. The truth of history lies only partially in history and entirely in man. Therefore, the meaning of the historical experience is to continuously make possible the dialogue of the human being with itself, a dialogue which takes place in a time called *historical communion*.

The universality of truths does not reside in the fact they reveal through dialogue a sense of time that we don't need to ask because we know it, as Saint Augustine put it: we know it because time is nothing else but us. Truths are universal because we exist in history; we are historical beings. To find the time communion in Plato's dialectics and in Aristotle's logic is the first concern of the present book. The author identifies some other places in the history of philosophy that could become relevant for this subject matter, exploring at the same time a few solutions given by thinkers which raised important questions about history and put the fundamental questions to the being: Henri Bergson, Martin Heidegger, Mircea Florian, Constantin Rădulescu-Motru, Immanuel Kant, and H. W. G. Hegel. Together with Plato, Aristotle, Parmenides or Heraclitus are the ones who offered me the opportunity to ask about the relationship between time and historical experience by confirming the perpetual dialogue of Platonic essence between philosophy and history. The key concepts of my discourse are truth, knowledge, freedom, time, creation, historical being, becoming, becoming into being, motion, change, circularity a.o.

The author of this text aims to spark readers' interest in the relationship between time and historical experience and encourage them to ask further questions on the topic. These pages have explored how time affects our experience of history as a fact of life.